I0411498

OBSESSIVE-COMPULSIVE-PHOBIAS

Introduction

If you've ever walked down a sidewalk, being careful not to step on the cracks, you have a form of obsessive, compulsive behavior. Almost everybody does. Most people, more or less, grow out of it. The old saying ", step on a crack, break your mother's back," which probably came from uneven sidewalks in earlier days could be part of what causes this. The Jack Nicholson movie, "As Good As It Gets", is a story of a man that has a much more active form of this behavior.

It's a subject I'm more than familiar with, having suffered several forms of this behavior for as far back as I can remember. The book entitled "Delivery of Love," by this author, tells the story of a man who successfully retires from his business in his early 30's. To fill his time, he becomes a volunteer for "Meals on Wheels". Being a volunteer myself, I fully understand the workings of this wonderful organization. They fill the needs of many people, mostly those up in years or disabled.

In the story, one client in the film is a young woman who hasn't dared to step out of her house in many years. Medical assistance, as well as food delivered to her by Meals on Wheels, sustains her day-to-day existence. Agoraphobia is one of the most extreme forms of obsessive- compulsive behavior. Her parents, who live close by, take care of any other needs she may have. The idea held by some, that this behavior can be easily rectified through psychiatry, is also dealt with in this book.

In my early years, dating back to elementary school and even before, I exhibited several forms of these compulsions. As I grew older, they became more powerful and developed into habits, many of which I still plague me at age 72.

The examples are many. As a young child, I kept yelling "good night" from my bedroom until my parents answered good night to me. In my early elementary school years, a form of reverse hiccup, annoyed my teachers and amused my classmates. I carried this behavior outside of the classroom as well.

Later in my junior high school years, now referred to as middle school, I had a compulsive jerking of my arms from my elbows. During that time, I wore a heavy jacket at school, even during the hottest days. Thankfully, I was able to ditch the jacket before getting into high school. At this time, it was discovered that I had epilepsy. I doubt this had anything to do with my behavior. I had four grand mal seizures in the next three years. At that point they stopped.

I began study on the violin during elementary school, and began a two to four hour daily practice regimen, which I maintained until ten years ago, when my arms began to give out. Both shoulders have since been replaced by titanium. This is not surprising as I hold the unofficial world's record of playing close to ten thousand violins and violas as a competition judge for the International Violin Makers Association. I suppose one could call that practice regimen a bit compulsive.

To this day, I cannot walk through a doorway without reaching around and touching both sides of the door before closing it. One might call this a habit, but in some cases, it's one that can't be helped. In our home, I have to look at either sides, touching the doorknob five times, or any other given number to satisfy this compulsion I may be going through. Several other forms are also bothersome. When I think about it, I will step on cracks in the sidewalk, however, one might call that a compulsion as well. Getting out of the car, and pulling the handle twice to be sure it's locked, and rubbing the back of my hand against the two doors on that side of the car twice, becomes very annoying when I realize I feel a need to have to do it. Hitting both sides of the faucet when getting out of a shower or at a sink, even when I consciously think about it, irritates me. I have seen myself consciously walk across the room if I forget to perform one of these rituals. Why? Who knows? On a happier note, a New Year's resolution was to stop these. Starting this book in the last month, I've been reasonably successful.

My cousin's wife always makes it a point to walk downstairs from the upstairs bedroom to check all doors and windows, even though she checked them before going up.

There are many other examples, too numerous to mention. I can imagine at this stage in life it may be one of the reasons I never married, even though, through my music, I enjoyed a rich social life with friends. I write this book in the hopes it may help someone, before this behavior becomes overwhelming for them.

Chapter 1

Linda McHugh had an extreme form of obsessive-compulsive behavior. It was a type of agoraphobia mentioned in the previous chapter.

Unfortunately, she didn't have parents to rely on. At age ten, she watched as a neighbor, whom her father had an altercation with the night before, brutally murdered her mother and father as they walked out their front door onto the porch. Linda screamed and slammed the door. When police arrived, they found her sitting, huddled in a corner with her arms around her knees, shivering.

Her older brother and his wife took her in. She was never comfortable going outside of their home. As time went on, it became more difficult for her to do this. For a short time, her brother drove her to school every morning and picked her up at night. It then became necessary for her to have a home tutor. Thankfully, her brother was a government employee and able to get state aid for her.

Her tutor, over the next few years, developed strong feelings for her, and she for him. She was eighteen years of age, and he was twenty-five. They were married after her graduation. She moved into his home, and for five years, never left the house.

Her husband, Steve, supported them through his work with the state. Attending at night, he got a degree in psychiatry at the University of Colorado. He had seen this form of behavior in other people through his work in the state offices. He realized Linda would need long-term psychiatric care for her condition. She was annoyed with this compulsion and, unlike many people with this condition, appreciated his help.

After getting her to make a move to the front porch, which he had screened in for that purpose, he set up a lawn swing inside the screened area to encourage her to come out of the house. After a short time, and many tries, Linda was finally able to come out. Steve left it at that for a couple of months. The next step would be a big one. He moved the mailbox from the porch to the street, and asked that she bring in the mail. For the first couple of weeks, he accompanied her. For a person in her extreme condition, this was a huge step forward. She was slowly able to overcome her compulsion over the next couple of years.

Steve found it easier for his wife to get out as time went by. He realized, she would have a form of this condition for many years, before recovering, if ever. But she was now happy with her life. She got a job at the city library, where she easily made many friends. An unhappy footnote to the story is that as she became less reliant on Steve, they slowly grew apart. He began seeing other women, and soon left her. One might think Linda would go back to her reclusive behavior. Fortunately, however, that didn't happen.

After a dark six-month period, her depression lifted and Linda began to date. Carl, one of the men working in the library, had a strong personality, which attracted Linda. Although a bit demanding, he was not mentally or physically abusive in any way. After her divorce was final, she and Carl were married in a civil ceremony and remained happily married, until her death at age 92.

Jean was a young woman just out of the military. She served four years in Afghanistan. After her release she checked herself into the VA hospital in San Diego. She had an anxiety that she couldn't control and it was getting worse. Doctors realized she had a form of PTSD as a result of being imprisoned by enemy insurgents where she was locked in a small room almost a month before help arrived. When she got home, she had a hard time leaving her house. The problem had gotten to the point where she was almost unable to get to the hospital. Medications and counseling brought that to a stop. Her Agoraphobic symptoms still exist but are now manageable.

Chapter 2

At an early age, Brian found, walking to and from school, he could not step on a sidewalk crack. He would also have to take just so many steps between them. He would walk, spacing four steps, unless the spaces were too far apart or too close together, in which case he would do steps in multiples of two. This habit, and more to come, soon became obsessive and part of his lifestyle. His parents began to notice idiosyncrasies, such as having all the books on his bookshelf lined up by size rather than title, which in itself could be classified as a bit obsessive. They also noticed that he insisted on stripping naked when going into the bathroom for any reason.

Other obsessive habits, such as folding the towels a certain way before placing them back on the rack, were soon found in the laundry basket after each use. They also noticed bars of soap wearing down faster and faster as time went on. Getting worried about this, they consulted the school psychologist who referred him to a board certified psychiatrist specializing in this condition. Her diagnosis was excessive-compulsive behavior or OCB.

After talking to Brian about this for a couple of hours, the psychiatrist realized she would not be much help to him. His habit of stripping naked in the bathroom at school was confined to the stall. He used a handicap stall, which was larger and had room for him to put his clothes aside near the rear of the stall. He did this, throughout his school years.

He spent many sessions over the years with a psychiatrist dealing in this behavior. He was not able to completely curb these habits. Over the years, he got to the point where he could not use a bar of soap more than one time. Luckily this progression was when he left his parents' home after high school. He was able to secure a job with the state and until getting married, maintained a relatively normal life.

It was only a matter of time before his new bride began to notice certain idiosyncrasies. He was careful not to perform them while he was around her. However, Gloria began to notice little things, such as towels she had folded, being changed to a different fold. He insisted on his and hers soap dishes. She began to notice his soap bar never wore down. His laundry was being changed several times a day. To his credit, he insisted on doing the laundry, as well as the dishes, vacuuming (always going in one direction) as well as other household chores, normally performed by the wife.

One might think this would make his wife ecstatic with joy. It soon began to wear on her. She began to look at her husband as a freak, rather than realizing he had a medical condition. She tried talking to him about this, but he would soon turn around and walk away from the discussion.

His behavior soon got the better of her. Gloria filed for divorce and moved into an apartment, alone. She had about all she could take of living with him. Thankfully, she married and enjoyed a perfect life with a dedicated slob. Unknown to her, this was at extreme opposite ends to Brian's behavior, and one which will be discussed in later chapters.

Brian decided against remarrying. This decision began to put him in an extremely depressed state. In the beginning he relished his newfound freedom. He was tired of walking on eggs, while around his wife. As time went on, his habits began to get the better of him. He developed several new ones; washing the bathroom and kitchen floors twice a day, even when not used, and washing windows each day.

Professional help did little to quell them. Neighbors noticed his car not being moved from his parking space. They observed newspapers piling up on the steps. This caused them to notify the police.

Brian was found in his bathtub full of blood from slashed wrists, along with a suicide note on the toilet seat, which read,

"The behavior, which I've endured over the years, has caused problems in my life too numerous to mention. It cost me my marriage, eventually my job, and now my sanity. I just can't take it any longer. I leave all my belongings to my ex-wife, and hope someday she can find it in her heart to forgive me for the misery I put her through; Brian."

Having been in that tub for several days, the smell in the room was not as bad as if he had been lying on the floor. It was still almost unbearable. Masks were worn by police officers, especially the detectives, and coroner's personnel. The body, which was not badly decomposed because of being submerged, was examined by forensics experts and then taken by the police to the corners office for autopsy.

Over the next couple of days the bathroom, as well as the rest of the house was scanned for forensic evidence of foul play. Neighbors were also questioned. After the autopsy, the coroner's office was satisfied that Brian's death was a result of suicide. The case was put to rest.

Chapter 3

A condition known as screw velocity has been responsible for misery in many people. It is a mortal fear of committing sin. Many people within the religious community suffer from it. The fear of retribution by God has caused many problems and deaths throughout history.

John Lewis suffered from this condition. He was not a terribly religious man, however he felt it his duty a stop sin in all forms. It started innocently enough telling neighbor's children across the fence, to stop using foul language. He began to feel an abnormal power over them causing his condition to escalate.

Being a man with a lot of strength in his hands, from construction work, he began chastising some of his fellow workers for their obscene language. He found telling them about it was not enough. He soon got physical with them. He lost many jobs because of this.

Within a years' time he was seeking out people committing, what he considered, sins. He began in some of the slum areas near his home in Youngstown, Ohio. In his mind, people living on the street were responsible for poor economic conditions as money going to them should have been used for the benefit of the entire city. Problems began when police were being called to the slum areas with greater degrees of frequency. Beatings, given some of these people, became more and more brutal.

John had taken it on himself to try, in any way necessary, to put a stop to any form of what he considered sin. These sins, started with profane language, then escalated to any number of actions he deemed sinful. Police were soon finding dead corpses lying around the various areas of the city. A couple of teenage kids were found dead in the park, beaten to death while sitting on a park bench. The two were dating and had stopped in the park for a "make out session". Thinking this was a precursor to premarital sex, John decided they should be taught a lesson before they went any farther. Although he had not intended to kill them, he felt no remorse.

John felt his actions were justified in these and the other killings. The police had other ideas. He was now classified as a serial killer. Having a degree of intelligence, he realized he had a lot of work to do in this city, however, felt he'd be wise to leave and continue his work somewhere else. He relocated to Newark New Jersey.

Within a short time, police were being called out to construction sites finding dead bodies, most of them killed with a knife. They began finding crosses carved into their foreheads. It didn't take long for them to realize there was a serial killer in their midst.

They realized the person committing these crimes was becoming more brazen with each kill. Where the killings had originally been done in the evening hours after work, police began finding bodies in various parts of the city during the daytime as well. As in most killings of this nature, the signature was always the same. Because of this, the authorities had not tied John to the murders in Youngstown.

In John's case, reality never lived up to his fantasy. This is true in most cases involving serial killers. He began to notice, his killings leading the evening news. He realized he would not be able to keep up here much longer and felt it wise to relocate again. He decided on the West Coast.

John's plane landed in San Francisco late in the evening the next day. He had heard of relaxed conditions on the West Coast; however it was worse than what he had been told. He had come to the city of New Age Thinking. John was not happy with what he saw. Most repulsive to him, were the gay communities throughout the city. He took it on himself, to clean up the "sins" that seemed to surround him everywhere he went. He decided to start on the streets.

John felt he had a lot to do and would therefore get rid of the evidence as he continued his mission. Most of his "service" to the city would be taken on under the cover of darkness. He had found a well-paying job on one of the new high-rises in the middle of the city. He found a piece of property outside the city that was ideal for his purposes. He began taking his handiwork out to the site and burying them in a mass grave. The disappearance of these people, both men and women, went unnoticed, for a short time.

The police soon realized they had a problem. John was not particular about who he picked up. Many of these street people had families. Their disappearance began being noticed. Police dragnets, as well as extra patrol units, were being utilized throughout the city. Because of the crosses carved in the foreheads, they soon realized these killings were done by one person. They had a serial killer in their midst. Although John felt like the proverbial kid in a candy store, he realized his actions in the city were soon to become a thing of the past.

As is the case of most serial killers, John became careless and was soon identified through surveillance cameras which had been set up citywide. Knowing the police were after him, he packed his bags. The next morning police were waiting at the door of his apartment as he walked out with a packed bag. He was taken into police custody.

John was taken into an interrogation room where he freely admitted to what he had been doing. Possibly going for an insanity plea, he began telling the detectives about his activities in other cities. In all, he had beaten or killed close to two hundred people. When asked to plead guilty or not guilty, John proudly admitted to what he had done. He told the judge, he'd done the city a service. Fortunately, the judge didn't see it that way. John was committed to a hospital for the criminally insane.

The majority of these cases are perpetrated by religious zealots throughout the world. In some cases, especially in the Middle East, this type of behavior can actually be encouraged, especially by their governments. It is a known fact that more people have died in the name of religion throughout history, than any other single cause. Many wars have been fought for the same reasons.

Chapter 4

Robert Warren was on leave from his job as a systems analyst for a large corporation. He was a man in his 20s and had not married. He was enjoying a sunny afternoon in a nearby Park when he witnessed a curious event. He watched as a man, carrying a leash, approached a young girl of about nine years of age. He couldn't be sure but felt it was probably a ruse concerning a lost puppy, or something that convinced the girl to go with him. He watched as the man put the girl in the back of a black van.

Feeling something was amiss, he was able to record the man's license number. He borrowed a cell phone from one of the kids in the park. He called 911 giving them a clear description of the van as well as its license number. He gave his name and address to the 911 operator as she requested. He also explained to her that he had borrowed the cell phone.

When getting home that afternoon, he got a call from the National City Police Department in San Diego. Detective John Bailey thanked him for the information and asked that he might be available in a couple days for an arraignment in downtown San Diego. Bob Warren was happy to oblige. Detective Bailey picked Bob up at his National City home about a mile from the park.

Together they drove downtown for the arraignment. Walking into the courtroom, Bob saw the suspect sitting at a desk in front, with two well-dressed men. Bob took a seat, and detective Bailey went up and sat at the table on the other side of the isle. Bob recognized the man sitting with detective Bailey; an assistant district attorney, whose face had been in the paper more than once.

The bailiff asked everybody in the court to rise as the judge walked through a side door. Bob was told his testimony would be crucial in getting the man arraigned. The suspect claimed he'd stopped at the 7-11 on Broadway in Chula Vista for a cold drink. He claimed he hadn't noticed the child in the back of the van, whose hands had been tied and her mouth duct taped.

With Bob's testimony, the man was arraigned on one count of kidnapping. Jack Bonner's attorneys asked for a speedy trial, which was his constitutional right. That was a mistake on their part. John Bailey began digging into other cases involving missing children over the last couple of years. As he dug deeper, Bonner began to look more like a seasoned kidnapper, than a first time offender.

He found there had been twelve missing children that were abducted in various parks around the county and never found. Seven were in the cold case files. Up to this point, the offender had never been seen. As no bodies had ever turned up, he checked with the police departments in Tijuana and Rosarito Beach, on the other side of the Mexican border.

Within the two cities there had been a total of ten girls between the ages of four and eight who had been sexually abused, killed and dumped. All the girls were of Hispanic origin, causing the Mexican police to assume they were all from Mexico. Fortunately, they had been buried in a Catholic Church yard rather than cremated. The other two girls were never found.

The remains of the ten girls were sent to the San Diego county coroner for autopsy. The semen recovered from two of the girls proved to be that of Jack Bonner. Both had been recent. It's questionable the man had experienced feelings of guilt, more likely the killings excited him. He eventually got sloppy as most offenders do.

Although Bonner's attorneys tried every trick in the book to get their client off, Bob warren's testimony, along with that of the coroner's office, left little doubt as to their client's guilt. He was found guilty on ten counts of kidnapping and first-degree murder.

A psychiatrist called in at the sentencing hearing, testified that Bonner was not insane at the time of the kidnappings however; suffered from a severe form of obsessive- compulsive behavior. Although semen had been found, his obsession turned out to be the terror he saw in the eyes of his victims as he strangled them.

Bonner had a happy home life. He had an attractive wife and three young children. They were between the ages of five and ten. His wife was totally unaware of the activities of her husband, and filed for divorce immediately after the trial.

Through a plea agreement, Jack Bonner admitted to the kidnapping and murder of the other eight girls. He was sentenced to life in a hospital for the criminally insane, which he would never leave. It had been explained to him that in a federal prison he wouldn't have lived more than a few months. Child offenders seldom do.

After the trials were over, Bob Warren was invited to lunch with John Bailey. While at lunch, John told Bob that he was to be given an award by the San Diego Police Department. Bob asked that his name and picture not be published by the newspaper. They honored that request. Two weeks later Bob Warren was given that award at a ceremonial dinner.

As a footnote, Bob noticed he was getting a lot more attention from young women he had been dating. A year later, one of these girls would become his wife.

Denny McFarland was a man in his 40s who had developed a fascination for girls under the age of ten. He forced oral sex and on many girls, telling his victim he would kill her as well as her parents if she said anything to them. This compulsion didn't start until later in life when Denny was in his late 30s. He had married young, and fathered two girls. The girls came home early one night and caught their mother in bed with another man. She soon divorced Denny. Neither of his daughters had any respect for him or his wife afterwards.

They felt their father was partially to blame. Neither girl would have anything to do with him and soon left home. Denny was a social drinker but never let it get out of hand until after the divorce. He would now often go into a drunken rage. It was at that point he would go hunting, finding his prey in parks, streets, and on playgrounds after school.

He began getting careless. He was spotted by a district attorney who was having lunch in a café across the street from an abduction. After news of his arrest, several of the children's parents started coming forward. He was convicted of twenty-five counts of child rape.

Chapter 5

In a small town, outside of Billings Montana, a body was found in a wooded area, with the eyes missing. Whoever performed this heinous crime apparently had no surgical skills. It looked like they had been cut out with a hunting knife.

Arriving on the scene, police officers got sick to their stomach as they noticed blood had poured out of the eye sockets. This told investigators the young man had been killed there.

Gary Robinson was the son of one of the merchants in town. As captain of the football team, he was popular with the school students. Police could find no reason for him to have been killed this way. This would be the first in a long line of similar killings throughout this area of Montana.

As sloppy as the perpetrator of these surgeries was, he was, by no means, sloppy in the way he kept crime scenes. The murders were all committed where the bodies were found. People committing these type crimes, the majority of who are men, are called Innucleators. They have an obsession with eyes. In most cases, their trophies are used for food. Eyes begin to deteriorate after a short time. In formaldehyde they may last longer, but not much.

Police detectives realized, given the wooded areas around the city, this perpetrator would not be easy to catch. These areas seemed to be a comfort zone for whoever was guilty of these crimes. The fact that most of these offenses were committed several weeks apart made it impossible for police to patrol all of these areas. In most cases the victims could not be seen from the highway.

Several leads had been phoned into the police, all turned out to be dead ends. It was a frustrating time for police detectives, as they had nothing to go on. The crimes had been going on for about eight months before the police finally caught a break.

A hunter in the woods came by a man being strangled. He shot his gun toward the perpetrator, who then ran out of the woods. The hunter, Ron Johnson, called 911. Police and an ambulance were soon on the scene. Ron hadn't seen the car, but told police it sounded like a muscle car.

In the hospital, Frank Elliott gave a police artist a pretty good description of the man who had attacked him. Although he just saw the man's face briefly before he was turned around and stabbed in the back, he said it was a face he would not soon forget.

The artist's rendering was given to the press throughout the area. This artist's conception appeared on the front page of all the newspapers in the area the next day. The man was identified later that morning by several people calling in. Police detectives arrived at the home of Lawrence Tahoe. Police surrounded the home, but the suspect wasn't there. Detective Steve Ramsey went into the kitchen, where he found a set of eyes in the refrigerator. That was pretty much all the evidence they found, but it was more than enough.

A photograph shown to Elliot in the hospital, confirmed Lawrence Tahoe as the man who attacked him.

He was seen in a motel 100 miles away. Police surrounded the room, taking him into custody. He was tried, convicted on eighteen counts of murder and sentenced to death by lethal injection.

It's difficult to say what causes compulsions of this nature. In Tahoe's case, his father lost an eye to disease. His father requested his lost eye be sterilized and coated with plastic. He then put it in a plastic case and placed it on the living room mantle in their home. Whether this action could be blamed for Lawrence's behavior, may never be fully understood.

Chapter 6

A compulsion that some people have is the desire to skin their victims alive. A form of torture, it's a need for human skin. It's more pliable and useful if it comes from a live person rather than a corpse. This can be done but usually requires the victim to be sedated. One such case was Franklin Moore. He was a haberdasher in Deadwood, South Dakota. His Highline coats were made from human skin. Because of their lightweight they were popular. Most of his victims were visitors without families, passing through town. He had a process for tanning the hides and artificially coloring them, for his desired effect. He started out innocently enough, using animal skins from a local ranch.

Within a period of time he graduated to using human corpses. He began to be obsessed with his newfound ideas. Because of their suppleness, he reasoned live humans would be best for this process.

The first was Janine, a woman in her 30s. She was driving through town on her way home from a family reunion. Because of the notoriety of Deadwood, she decided to drive through it. Franklin met her in the lounge of her hotel. This was where he met the majority of his victims.

The next morning in the garage at the hotel, he overpowered her. He took her and her car to his nearby home, on 5 acres, just out of town.

There he changed the plates and the VIN number. He would later sell the car on the black market in Sioux Falls.

The car was secondary to his plan. He took Janine into one of the outbuildings on the property. There, he knocked her out and proceeded to skin her alive. After killing her, he treated the skin and began the tanning process. It would take at least two complete skins to complete a coat depending on its size.

Before being caught, he was somehow able to get away with this for almost a year. During that time he had killed and skinned forty-six men and women. Although this venture was for profit, Franklin was ruled incompetent to stand trial, and spent the rest of his life in a hospital for the criminally insane, in Sioux Falls.

There have been several cases in history of this type of behavior. In many cases it may never be understood what brought on this problem. Some of the people brought up on these charges testified it was sexual pleasure and gratification that caused this. In some cases skin from their victims would be tightly wrapped around the perpetrators male organ giving them heightened pleasure. In some cases the skin would even be glued onto their phallus before having sex. Perhaps this was an attempt to enhance their partner's pleasure. Who knows?

Chapter 7

Another obsession that strikes fear in the heart of man is a condition known as the Renfeld syndrome. The name is derived from Graham Stokers famous novel, Dracula. The folklore of vampires has been around since before the dawn of history. Although considered imaginary, there are many cases of people taking the blood of others to drink. Some South American tribes used human blood in sacrifice to the gods.

In earlier years, many people thought vampires could be killed by a stake being driven through their heart. Images of vampires with fangs have also emerged over the years. These go back to the days of Transylvania, centuries ago.

Unfortunately, the fascination with this type of behavior has worked its way into compulsions by certain members of the human race. One such person was Eugene Phillips. His attraction to this behavior began at an early age. It began with a boy curious about the blood of animals. It started with a bird he had found in the forest by his home in Eureka, California.

The bird was unable to fly because of a broken wing. Eugene pulled the head off the bird. It began to bleed as he watched. As the blood came out, he put it to his mouth and began to taste and then drink it. That started a fascination with him that would not be quelled until he was caught many years later.

This became an obsession for him. Unfortunately, this behavior didn't stop at birds. He soon graduated to other members of the animal kingdom. Stray cats abounded in the neighborhood, and became the best source of his newfound addiction. This continued on through his teen years. Although members of his middle and high school had no idea of this obsession, they never warmed up to him. After graduation he went to medical school, specializing in veterinary medicine.

Working in an animal shelter in nearby Arcata, California, he had a vast amount of animals that were being put down each week. Volunteering for this duty gave a much needed supply to feed his addiction. It wasn't long before the obsession overcame him. Although starting out cutting himself, and licking his own blood off his arms, he soon graduated to drawing his blood with hypodermic needles.

Authorities were called to a walking path behind Humboldt State University in Arcata. The victim lay in a clump of trees, puncture wounds in his neck. The victim, Mary Louise Bellingham, had been dead for almost 12 hours. Students from the University, on an early morning hike, discovered the body and called police. This would be the first in a rash of similar murders reaching as far north as Crescent City.

A week later a second body was found on clam Beach, about ten miles from the University. This time the victim was an older man. He had been beaten, and violated by the perpetrator using fang like teeth.

The county coroner thought these were probably made of plastic, ordered through a mail order catalog on the Internet. It's amazing the things one can buy online.

Police felt that the murder had been committed sometime during the night as the body was in the first stages of rigor mortis. An autopsy showed the man had been subdued, and then beaten to death after the blood had been drained from his body. Had he been killed before hand, the attacker would have had a much harder time committing this atrocious act, as the heart would have stopped pumping blood.

Police realized the person involved in these murders was a serial killer. Over the next few weeks seventeen new bodies had been discovered. The crimes showed no differentiation in sex, nor were any of the victims sexually violated. All were killed by blunt trauma, most of them beaten into helplessness before the act. There was no known motivation to any of these vicious crimes outside the obvious nourishment, if not pleasure, derived by the perpetrator.

The FBI was called in, even though the crimes had not crossed the Oregon border. Whether this was done by accident or design was not known. As in most cases of serial killers, Eugene was no exception. He slipped up leaving fingerprints on a board he had used to kill his latest victim, Jonathan Ross.

At Eugene's home in Eureka, police found small bottles of blood in the refrigerator. The blood turned out to be human. Unfortunately, newspaper headlines had mentioned his fingerprints on the board found by police. A stakeout was ordered on his home but authorities realized he would probably not return. Those fingerprints were not the only thing Eugene had slipped up on. It was almost as if he wanted to be caught. His credit card statements from the bank led police right to Ashland Oregon.

Oregon State police apprehended the suspect in an apartment building next to the University, just outside of town. He went peacefully and was extradited to Eureka, where he stood trial for multiple counts of first-degree murder. He was tried and sentenced to life in a state mental facility with no possibility of parole.

This behavior is uncommon in women. There have been cases when a prostitute (or a wife, or girlfriend) has been asked by a man to bite them hard on the neck, approximating that of a vampire. In many cases blood can be drawn, however this can be an extremely dangerous practice as the carotid artery resides there. There have been more than a few deaths in recorded history as a result of this. Blood rather than pain is usually, but not always, the motive.

Although this type of behavior is highly uncommon, it does exist especially in cults. It's not unusual for signs of the devil to be carved in blood on trees throughout areas of the country. These rituals usually involve animal blood. There has been a rise in this type of crime, but so far it's just been proportionate to the rise in population. As long as man lives on this earth, there will always be a certain fascination by some people, to this type of behavior.

Francois Bardot was an artist living in Paris in the 19th century. From the time he was five years old, seeing his brother bleeding from an accident with a double hung window, he became obsessed with blood.

After art school at the Louvre, he decided to take his art to a different level, using his fascination with blood.

He began doing abstract art using the blood of animals. As time went on he felt he needed to improve on his techniques. He began experimenting using the blood of human corpses. It may never be known why he decided to graduate to live victims.

His art was praised throughout Paris as being something fresh. It was that. He used the blood of prostitutes which he lured to his apartment. This went well, until he picked the wrong one. He had always put a mask over the face of his victims in which he had put drugs to make them unconscious. He would then drain a couple of pints of the blood, leaving just enough for them to survive.

This technique was not discovered until one these girls died. He had never counted on this and was caught when trying to dispose of the body. He was tried for murder, and hanged.

This is not the only time this technique had been tried, in fact during the dark ages and before, this had been done by several artists, including a French king.

Bardot's paintings increased in notoriety, driving the prices way up. As in many cases, he died before seeing the impact his paintings had on the art world.

Chapter 8

A condition, mostly inherent to women, is a strong desire to keep company with violent men. Hybristophilia is not uncommon in our society. There are many cases of women falling in love with, and in some cases marrying men on death row. This type of obsessive behavior is hard for most people to understand. It probably dates back to our ancestors. Many women were attracted to alpha males, because they felt protected by them. In this day and age it's hard to comprehend this type of reasoning.

Selena Barra was a young woman in her mid-30s. Although her father did not abuse her sexually, he ruled over the household with a firm hand. From her earliest childhood she witnessed her mother being subservient to her father's wishes. This would later form an obsession for her.

She began, quite innocently, writing letters to inmates at the state prison. Friends and family applauded her for this. As time went on, these letters became more and more frequent. They say all that is worth doing, is what we do for others.

She began using e-mail when it became popular. In this fashion, inmates could return her letters. This became a daily ritual for her. In some cases, she was writing and answering up to ten a day. It was easy to see that some of these men were jailed for violent crimes. These were the ones that attracted Selena the most. She soon began to quit answering all those sent to her except by inmates on death row.

One particularly violent man, Frank Escobar, scheduled to be put to death the following year, was imprisoned for mass murder. His crime sprees started when he was ten years old, killing animals for no particular reason. In his early teens he became a gang member, and worked his way up to leading one of these gangs. He later graduated to killing men and women alike, for no reason. The law finally caught up with him as he shot and killed a clerk in a local liquor store. Unfortunately, for him, he was caught on a video camera.

The attention he was paying Selena caused her to develop deep feelings for him. On a weekly basis she began taking the bus the two hundred miles to the prison. She soon changed jobs and moved into an apartment building close to the prison so she could visit him daily. It was uncertain why prison officials allowed this, however these visits were strictly guarded. The couple decided to marry several months later. The marriage was never consummated.

On the night of his execution, Selena was in the viewing room in tears as the needle went into his arm. After the execution she left the room in hysterics. The prison physician gave her a shot to calm her down. It was unclear exactly what she expected to see. The following morning, she walked in front of a taxicab. Although she wanted to die, she wound up a paraplegic. Why? Who knows?

According to psychiatrists, there are several reasons for this type of behavior. One, as in her case, was a desire for a father figure, as hers had died several years before. A popular reason is to change the guy into whatever she thinks she wants.

In some cases the woman sees the man as a little boy who needs her help. In other cases the person is looking for the media spotlight. This is one wish the media is only too happy to grant. In cases like this, they may dig into her life from early childhood.

All of these women, for the most part, come from insecure backgrounds. Another popular reason is that the woman always knows exactly where her husband is. In this instance it seems to be more a case of protecting herself from a more normal marriage. This is considered probably the worst case of insecurity. Unfortunately, this type of condition makes it almost impossible for a woman to enjoy a more fulfilling life with a husband and children.

Gary Broderick was married to Gail for five years before committing cold-blooded murder in a liquor store he was holding up. He was tried and convicted of first-degree murder. As the death penalty didn't exist in that state, he was given life without parole. Gail had no children and remained unmarried. Her friends tried to get her interested in divorce from Gary and regain a social life, but she refused.

Her friends thought she was foolish and tried more than once to set her up with a man. She refused their offers telling them she was a married woman and had no intention of changing that. Her friends finally gave up trying. She knew exactly where her husband was and felt he would always be faithful to her for that reason. In their five years of marriage Gary had several sexual encounters outside of the marriage. In truth, she was terribly insecure and married at an early age coming out of a violent childhood. Not wanting to take a chance on a re-performance was her motivation to stay single. She seldom called or visited him in prison, but remained faithful until she died at age sixty-five. Gary found all the sexual satisfaction he needed by other inmates in the prison.

Chapter 9

Abe Brickman fell into the category of a profiler – psychopath. That's a polite word for a con artist. This often becomes an obsession, which some people are unable to stop. Abe was one of these. He began, quite innocently, selling shares of stock in a defunct company. He didn't realize it at the time. However, he never considered reimbursing the money to his clients.

Realizing this may be an easy way to make a living, he decided to give it a try. His first move was to a more affluent community. He decided on Fort Lauderdale, Florida.

Working under the assumed name of Robert Carlisle, he began picking up checks from wealthy women to invest for them. Being a good looking guy, and quite the charmer, he was taking these women for larger and larger sums of money. Many of these checks amounted to well over a hundred thousand dollars. He soon had several clients throughout the city, wining and dining them on a regular basis. In some cases he worked his way into their bedrooms as well.

After several months he began feeling the heat. Although some of the women felt the fringe benefits were well worth the investment, some did not. Linda Forsyth hired her attorney to look into Roberts practices. Within a couple of days, they went to the police. Abe got wind of this and decided to pick up stakes. During his stay in Florida he had made close to a million dollars.

In Hollywood, California, he used another assumed name, Reginald Barton. He felt the name would give him class. He got a California driver's license and I.D. He completely changed his appearance, growing a beard and mustache, and having his hair dyed.

The film industry has many wealthy people. One of these was a gentleman, sixty years of age, William Masters. He had put together a sizable portfolio as a director for a number of years in soap operas. Much of this was liquid. He and Reginald became friends in one of Hollywood's nightspots. The two began a business relationship that lasted a number of months. During this time Masters was able to convince several of the leading Hollywood stars to invest with Reginald.

Portfolios, as well as websites, showed Barton to be a legitimate businessman involved in investments throughout the world. Over drinks one evening, he was able to convince Masters of a huge project he was putting together in Hong Kong. This involved the construction and management of a sixty story luxury hotel, overlooking the water. These plans had been put together for him by a firm in Austin Texas.

Between William Masters and twelve other investors, "Reginald" was able to increase his overseas account by more than five million dollars. He pulled up stakes overnight, leaving ten people wondering what had happened. He hailed a taxi, taking him to a bus station, and then onto John Wayne Airport in Orange, California. He was constantly tripping over his ego.

His next victims were in a posh area just outside of Portland Oregon. Under the name Floyd Cabrillo, he began working scams throughout the area.

Lynn Warren was a wealthy, petite redhead in her early 30s. She had divorced her wealthy husband when she caught him playing the field. Some of these girls her husband was picking up off the streets. In court, she was awarded a good part of his fortune. She moved to Portland from Great Falls, Montana.

Lynn met Floyd at a cocktail lounge in one of the large hotels just outside of Portland. He could smell money the minute she sat next to him. After talking a few minutes, the two moved over to a booth for more drinks and conversation. He told her that he had put an investment group together to buy, and then renovate, a large hotel in Portland. He told her he was still close to a quarter million dollars short of the goal. He was careful not to ask her for money. That would come later.

Floyd told her he had just gotten out of a messy divorce himself. Over the next couple days, he wined and dined her. Within the week, they began spending nights together. Although he maintained his hotel room, most of these nights were spent at her home. It was a large cabin like home, overlooking a beautiful lake.

It didn't take long for him to work his way into her heart, as well as her bank account. She told him she was invested in stocks and bonds. The quarter million dollars she gave him took most of her savings in the bank. The prospectus he showed her, and her attorney, convinced them both. Walt Masterson her attorney, put up a hundred thousand dollars of his own. He started giving Floyd new clients as well.

Floyd had put together a sizable portfolio by the time everything was said and done. He shaved off the beard and mustache he had grown before going to Oregon, as well as dying his hair. He barely recognized himself. He pulled up stakes with another two million dollars. The website he had used in Florida, and the one in Oregon, were both cancelled. He built a new website before going to Montréal Canada.

Under the name, Jack Edelman, he moved into a posh hotel in Montreal. Within days he found several marks. Most of these were wealthy divorcees or widows, and were not sophisticated in business dealings. For the most part, they let their attorneys or professional managers take care of their portfolios.

The first of these was Loretta Parson. Her husband had given her a generous divorce settlement which would take care of her for the rest of her life, and then some. The settlement amounted to close to five million dollars. It was not long before she and Jack were an item. She had stars in her eyes. He had dollar signs in his. It took about a week for Jack to gain her confidence. Her attorney and business manager were not quite so easy to convince. Jack decided to take his time and try to gain their confidence as well. He set up a dummy corporation showing large amounts of assets, which most competent attorneys should have seen through. Unfortunately Loretta's had not.

On the sly, Jack had been seeing other women in various parts of town. Using short business trips as an excuse, he was able to hide his indiscretions from all of them. He cleared the area with a total of three million dollars. He had his money in an overseas bank account, which, with interest, totaled close to eleven million dollars.

He flew to London, England where he used the same scam as he had in the United States and Canada. He began building a reputation for himself. He was able to have various documents forged, showing him to be an upstanding businessman.

With the money he now had, he was able to dress in upscale clothes, and stay at the most luxurious hotels in London. He was able to find wealthy clients, both men and women in the lounges of these hotels. With his bank account now totaling twenty million dollars plus, he flew to New York.

Making more money was now his only obsession. He could care less how he got it, as he had no conscience. He had used so many aliases; he began to get them mixed up. This was his downfall. In two cases, in New York, he murdered his clients. This was done, when another client realized he was using a false name. Because of this, as well as the police realizing he was a scam artist, the FBI was called in. Within a couple of months, Abe was in custody.

Although he was able to afford the best legal team money can buy, he was sentenced to life without parole at the federal penitentiary in Leavenworth Kansas. His bank account was seized and the money returned to his clients. It has been said that gratitude is a burden, however revenge is a pleasure.

In the modern world the compulsion or obsession in many people to gain wealth takes a priority over their families. The divorce rates among these men and women are high. Common among many of the men in this category is marrying much younger women to help their ego; hence the high divorce rate among them. There are a lot of Abe's out there fleecing money from unsuspecting individuals, both men and women. This works both ways.

Sandy Felix was an extreme con artist that always went by an assumed name. She was able to fleece several men out of their money as well as respect. She would find a man in a nightclub or hotel lounge. She always made sure they were either divorced or single. At that point she would make overtures to the guy. She saw to it these never led to her bedroom claiming to save herself for marriage. She was able to con him out of diamonds, jewelry and anything else she felt she could get away with. Leading him on to believe marriage was on the horizon, she was able to gain their respect and devotion, as well as expensive gifts.

Sandy had no intention of going beyond the con. Her pet trick was to set herself up as the victim of either a car or gun. She could've cared less if one of her victims tried to substantiate her death. By that time she had fled to another state.

Chapter 10

A condition most common in men is an overwhelming desire to seek sexual gratification with an unwilling partner. These rapes are more common than most police departments are willing to admit. In some cases this may amount to an overaggressive boyfriend or husband. In many cases it becomes a compulsion. This is known as Biastophilia. In most instances these acts are performed by men from their 20s to their 50s. Unfortunately, many are never reported.

David St. John was a twenty-five-year-old man who suffered from this condition from the time he was eighteen. His spree began just after high school. In this form of Biastophilia, there is no desire to kill or maim the victim. David had a domineering mother, which is the case in many people suffering from this. He always wore a mask, covering facial features, as well as lifts in his shoes to make him appear taller than his 6 foot frame. He would always burn his clothes after committing one of these atrocities. He had been born to a middle-class family in New Hampshire, and at age 15 the family had moved to Kansas City, Missouri, where his father took a job at the General Motors plant there.

A woman ten years his senior was his first victim. Greta was a grad student at UMKC. She was suddenly and viciously attacked by David while spending a leisurely evening near the zoo at Swope Park. He had no desire whatever to kill her however he derived most of his gratification, not so much from the sex act, as the violence involved. The fear in his victim's eyes is what drove him. Luckily for him, he had the good sense to use a condom and gloves as well as the mask.

After the attack Greta was able to call the police and they summoned an ambulance to her position. She was taken to the hospital in extreme trauma, having suffered a black eye and a broken nose in the attack. Unfortunately, she was unable to give police much information.

Although there had been several attacks in the park, this was the first one that left no evidence. David always left his car parked at least a mile from his potential attack. Various parks around the city became his venues.

Laura Parker was his second victim found in a park on the other side of the city near the Kansas border. Here again she was violently raped and beaten. Again he left the police with just questions. Laura was taken to Memorial hospital, but her examination left no clues as to David's identity.

As time went on, David began being more efficient at his task. Some of his victims were coming into the hospital in near death. He began being more careful about the sites he was choosing. One of his more aggressive attacks was on the front lawn of the Nelson art gallery. His victims always lay where they were attacked. He had never bothered to move them to dump sites as they were left alive.

Getting sexual gratification was getting harder for David as these attacks went on. Within a few months these assaults were becoming more violent with each attack. He soon found the only way he could gratify his violent attacks, was to kill the victim. He went from serial rapist to serial killer within a couple of months. Because of this, the FBI was called in to help.

By a fluke, David was seen out in the woods early one evening by a hunter. When witnessing what was going on, Johnathan aimed the gun at David, and ordered him off his victim. As much as Jonathan wanted to put a bullet through David's head, he resisted, calling the police instead. When the police got there David's head had been bashed in by Jonathan's gun stock.

David was taken to Truman Medical Center where he was treated for a concussion, along with other injuries. He was tried and convicted on twenty counts of rape and five counts of first-degree murder. David was found mentally incompetent to stand trial and was sentenced to life without parole in a state mental hospital.

In many cases, like David's, the sex act itself becomes secondary to violence and pain inflicted on the victim. In most instances the perpetrators are caught within months of their first act, before they resort to murder, in order to bring satisfaction to themselves.

*****

Breanne Jackson was a college student in the Midwest. One night at a frat party, she and her older sister, Leslie, went their separate ways. Leslie noticed her being taken in another room, willingly. Later, not being able to find her sister, Leslie went back to the apartment the two girls shared. She found Breanne passed out on the swing in the front yard. Her breath smelled of whiskey. Leslie immediately called 911 when she couldn't revive Breanne. They took her to the hospital where she went into a coma. She died two hours later of acute alcohol poisoning.

Knowing her sister wasn't a heavy drinker, Leslie was shocked when doctors told her that Breanne would've had to drink a quart of scotch in order to show the high blood alcohol levels she had. They had also found evidence of rape by at least three men. Leslie became incensed by this.

A friend in the police department gave her the names of the three men. She lured them to her home. One at a time she was able to first drug them and then drag them down the stairway to the basement. There they were bound and gagged. When the three refused to admit their involvement, Leslie pistol whipped them and then shot them in the head.

Afterward she dragged them upstairs to her van. Late that night she took them to the police station downtown. A security camera caught her as she deposited the bodies on the lawn in front of the station.

The next morning police showed up at her front door. She waited for them to pick her up. In court, she freely pled guilty to the murder of the three men. The jury felt sympathy for her when her attorney explained what had taken place. The jury, reluctantly, found her guilty of second degree manslaughter. The judge ordered a psych evaluation. The next day Leslie was sentenced to ten years in a mental hospital. She is now serving that sentence.

*****

Another case similar to Leslie's was reported in a town outside of Portland Oregon. James Brown's younger sister, Sherry, was found drugged, raped and in a severe coma. An ambulance picked her up at her apartment and raced her to a nearby emergency room. She died five days later. An autopsy showed she had been gang-raped. Five men were taken into custody when their DNA showed up in the girl's body. They were released when their families put up the bail. All believed in the innocence of their sons. James Brown did not share in that belief.

One by one he stalked the boys, grabbing them when he could. He took them out to a deserted barn in a wooded area. There he stripped them naked in front of each other, and proceeded to kill each, one by one.

After the deed was done, James left the state. The bodies were found by the property owner three weeks later, horribly decomposed. He notified police immediately. James Brown headed their list of suspects as soon as dental records identified the boys. An all-points bulletin was put out throughout the country.

Although James had changed his appearance he was still recognized through a photograph on the front page of the paper in Charlottesville North Carolina. He went to the local police station and gave himself up.

The judge and jury sympathized with him, but could not condone what he had done. He was charged with second-degree murder and given a life sentence in the state prison, with a possibility of parole in twenty years.

*****

Some might consider what he and Leslie had done as justifiable homicide. However we have laws in this country for a reason. When they're broken, it's the duty of the law to bring the perpetrators to justice. There are more than just a few of these kinds of cases being settled without the benefit of due process. The law will not turn a blind eye to these, although many are sent to cold case files.

Chapter 11

Erotic asphyxiation has been responsible for the deaths of many people over the years. Most are male, in their teens and early 20s. In some cases they had been performing this act for several months before making a fatal mistake.

In most cases sexual gratification, not suicide, is the predominant reason for committing this act. One of the first known cases of erotic asphyxiation was by the composer of the opera, "The battle of Prague", Frantisek Kotzwara. He hired a prostitute to cut off his testicles. She refused, however had sex with him while he had a rope around his neck. Whether or not he intended suicide is hard to say. The girl was tried for murder, but acquitted.

There are between five hundred and a thousand deaths attributed to erotic asphyxiation annually. In the majority of these cases, death is accidental.

Friedman Watson was a young man of twenty-four. He had been performing this act with his girlfriend, Molly, at his side. He had done this many times as a precursor to the sex act with her. As they continued this practice over a couple of years, she began to notice his need to hang from the rope, looped over his closet door, for longer periods of time. He found he could not attain sexual satisfaction without it. She became wary of his habits and left him.

Although at the time he didn't realize it, her leaving signed his death warrant. Continuing the practice, using masturbation, he continued to prolong his amount of time with a rope. Authorities found him hanging a week later, after neighbors noticed strange odors emanating from his apartment. An autopsy ruled his death suicide. Molly called authorities after seeing the story in the newspaper. She was called in to testify at a coroner's inquest. That ruling was changed to accidental death.

Bill Austin had never used a partner. He practiced this act solo. At the age of 16, he had read about this practice in an erotic magazine. He used a belt tied to a bed post. Using this method he got on his knees, naked, bending forward as the belt tightened around his neck. His parents found him the following morning. His hand remained tightly held around his penis and a large amount of seminal fluid on the floor in front of him. They had no idea their son had a problem of this nature.

*****

Fred Priestley was a man of twenty-five. He and his wife, Darla, belonged to a club that freely practiced all sorts of bizarre practices. Although predominantly a wife swapping club, many members practiced odd acts as a precursor to and during sex. While in the club they heard about the practice of erotic asphyxiation. As a couple, they decided to give it a try.

This act became a ritual. Although not implemented on every occasion of the sex act, it was becoming more and more frequent. Darla seemed to get as big a kick out of it as Fred. They continued this practice over a period of years, successfully. What they didn't realize was the danger of cutting off oxygen to the brain during the sessions.

Fred found he was becoming more forgetful all the time. By the time Darla realized this, Fred had serious problems with dementia, unusual for a man his age. Darla insisted they stop. They did this, but within a couple months Fred began to miss the thrill he got as he played with death. Darla found him dead, with a rope around his neck, in the den. Whether the chair he was standing on accidentally fell out from under him, or he pushed it, was never clear. His death was ruled a suicide.

Albert Williams was a young unmarried man with this obsession. He never wanted to get into a relationship because of it. He would often tie a rope around his neck and another to the top of his door. He made it a point to wear a harness he had made, and hook it to the top of the door to prevent strangling himself to death. He would slowly lower himself to a point right before unconsciousness. He would then perform the act of masturbation, bringing himself to orgasm before straightening up. He performed this act on a weekly basis. As he felt the need to expand this technique, he finally hung himself.

There have been many Hollywood actors such as David Carradine that have died this way accidentally, at their own hands. Many rock stars have succumbed to this as well. Probably a large reason for this is their desire for drugs and alcohol. When on these, the brain requires more oxygen than normal. For this reason many deaths occur, as the victims don't have the amount of time they normally do when sober.

Albert Dekker was found in his Hollywood home in the late 60s. He was found naked, kneeling in his bathtub with a rope around his neck. In this strange case, he was found blindfolded, handcuffed and a ball gag in his mouth. Two hypodermic needles were in his arm. There were words and drawings in lipstick all over his body. Was it suicide?

Albert Dekker was an outspoken critic of McCarthy during the hearings on communist behavior by the film industry in Hollywood. These were held in the early fifties. He was blacklisted and never worked in films again. Did he take his life because of this? We will probably never know.

Chapter 12

The compulsion for overeating results in a condition known as obesity. It's well-known that genetics and family can play a large role in this. Too often this is used as an excuse to over eat. Many of us that have this condition know only too well its ramifications. Finding it harder and harder to get out of bed in the morning, sore feet, and the lack of self-worth, are some of its results. Some people find overweight individuals to be attractive, most do not. It is a problem that has become all too common throughout the world today.

Our lifestyle is becoming more and more sedentary as computers come into our lives. Although there has been an upsurge in the use of gymnasiums, worldwide, all too often many people quit after thinking they've gotten enough out of it. Another large reason for obesity in this country, and now in many others, are the drive-in, fast food restaurants.

*****

Laura Evans works as an attorney's assistant in a large law firm in downtown Cincinnati. As her schedule became more hectic, she tended to let her husband worry about feeding and getting the kids off to school in the morning. She "just grabs something on the way". After her first child, she joined a gym, and managed to keep her figure till the second one came along. At that point she got busy. After seven years of marriage she has become overweight, weighing in at 255 pounds. For a woman 5'6" she is considered morbidly obese. With professional help she is beginning to correct the problem.

*****

Yang tin was ten years old when his family immigrated to the United States from China. Like most immigrants they came from other countries for a better life. His family members took jobs that most Americans would consider insignificant. His father, insisted his son go to school and then continue on to the University of California, San Francisco. They resided in an area called Chinatown. Yang, while in school, adopted the name Bert Smith, which his father did not approve.

After studying culinary arts at the University, Bert got a job as a chef in one of Chinatown's better restaurants. He was hard-working and knowledgeable. After five years, with his family's help, he was able to buy out the owner. During his tenure as head chef, the major part of his job was to taste everything cooked. They say people can resist anything but temptation. That's true when it comes to weight control, however one must eat.

His weight and girth slowly began to increase as time went on. This was surprising as genetics often plays a role. Other members of his family were trim and fit. His doctors encouraged him to take it easy at the table; however he became obsessed with eating. His weight had gone from one hundred and forty pounds in school to three hundred and twenty-five at age 35. A minor heart attack put a stop to this.

He began a diet of brown rice and vegetables, cooked in water. When hitting the weight of two hundred and fifty pounds, his doctors put him on an exercise program, involving walking and enjoying more activities. His weight began to drop more slowly as time went on.

Within a two-year period, his diet and exercise program put him at the hundred and sixty-five pounds he was shooting for. He had more energy, but the doctors wanted to keep an eye on him. Although the earlier heart attack considered minor, there was damage to his heart.

A major factor in obesity is nervousness. Some bite fingernails; some bite anything they can get into their mouth. As most any doctor will tell you, diets don't work. Although many of them are obese as well, they try to keep their patients as healthy as possible.

We all know people that have lived into their 80s and 90s being overweight all their lives, but the majority succumbed to heart attacks and other weight related health problems in their 40s and 50s, and earlier. Obesity coming on in the late stages of life can cause type II diabetes and other health ailments.

Obesity is now considered the largest health problem in the United States. Many billions of dollars are spent annually trying to correct this. Prescription drugs, as well as over-the-counter medications, to combat obesity, are sold by the millions.

*****

Bulimia is highly complex and greatly impacts a person's emotional and physical health. It is a compulsion to over eat and then vomit for no apparent reason. Many health spas promoting cures for this have popped up worldwide. Those running the spas realize that overweight people generally have underlying causes. These can include the death of loved ones, dismissal from a job, or a complete lack of feeling of self-worth. Of course most of us just like to eat, especially comfort foods.

Can one look at a poster or billboard without seeing a scantily clad girl wearing tank top and jeans? In the 80s, Twiggy was all the rage. Women of all ages wanted to look like her. Fashion models, who often vomit meals, find they have health problems as they get older because of this. In the nineteenth century, and before, overweight women were desired. Being affluent, they ate better than most of the populace.

Anybody looking at a Ruben's painting will notice the women in his paintings are quite portly. Of course in this modern day and age, this is no longer the case. Regardless of one's weight, good health should be the key factor in our behavior. Nutrition and exercise play a large role in our longevity as well.

Marty Wilson was a woman of forty-five. Like many women her age, she began getting a bit portly. At her doctor's advice, she finally got into an exercise program of walking and working out in the gym.

Unfortunately, she used these activities as an excuse to continue her habit of Overeating. In our culture, this is not terribly uncommon. As her weight was constantly on the rise, she discontinued seeing her doctor except when absolutely necessary. She saw to it these trips were few and far between, as she knew a lecture would ensue as soon as she walked into his office. It took a heart attack to make her realize the fallacy of her ways. She has now brought down her weight to a manageable level, and remains on her exercise programs.

Chapter 13

Fits of rage can occur in anybody from time to time. These can be caused by any number of reasons. Some people have tempers they cannot control and will often find themselves in trouble because of it. There's a saying "reason is not automatic; those that deny it cannot be conquered by it."

The problem with uncontrolled anger, which this author is often guilty of, can cause a lot of problems in their lives. Some people get mad at things and not at people, luckily I'm in that category. Anger towards others can sometimes be found in almost anyone. When this anger gets out of hand, a dangerous situation occurs. This is especially true behind the wheel of a motor vehicle.

Frank Fields was on his way home one night when he was cut off in traffic. He exploded, as he could see no reason for the other driver to be so careless. The thought that the other driver may not have seen him, didn't even cross his mind. He passed the car, side-swiping it off the road and into a tree alongside the road. He immediately sped away as it wasn't his fault; after all, the other driver started it, right?

The judge didn't see it that way. When he was apprehended, Frank was sentenced to fifteen years in prison for second-degree murder.

In a similar case, Johnny and Yolanda were out enjoying a drive. He was driving slower than the speed of traffic which infuriated Dick Morrow who was driving a heavy duty pickup truck behind them. When Johnny failed to move over, after Bill blew his horn repeatedly, he drove around to the right of them purposely hitting the front end of the young couple's car. This caused their car to go out of control over the center divider and into oncoming traffic, the couple along with two others in the approaching car, died at the scene.

The third person, their sixteen-year-old daughter, died in the hospital the next morning of massive head trauma. Luckily the car behind them witnessed this act and recorded the trucks license number.

Dick Morrow was convicted of vehicular manslaughter and sentenced to life in prison with no possibility of parole. As the judge at his trial said, "you may as well have killed them with a shotgun".

Although Morrow's case is an extreme example, it's not all that uncommon. Road rage has been around since the days of horse and buggy; however the advent of the automobile has made it deadly as well. Drive-by shootings, which will later be examined in this book, has nothing to do with road rage.

Mira Brunner was a young woman of sixteen, who had just gotten her driver's license. Her parents bought her, a compact car. Like many teens, her actions behind the wheel were not yet automatic. She had gotten into the bad habit of driving entirely too fast and too close to traffic ahead of her. Paul Nielsen and his wife Mandy were in the car directly in front of her. Paul was getting nervous and a little hot under the collar. Mandy, knowing Paul's temper, tried to keep her husband cool. His temper finally got the best of him. At 70 mph he slammed on the brakes of the large Cadillac he was driving. Mira was driving too fast and too close to be able to stop in time.

Paul and Mandy were not injured; however Mira was seriously injured when her airbag failed to explode. She was rushed to the hospital and recovered. Both arms were broken when she fell into the steering wheel. She was cited for reckless driving. His reason for the sudden stop was explained by an imaginary bird flying into the windshield. When Mandy failed to say anything, Paul was off the hook. As the saying goes "one who doesn't punish evil, commands it to be done". This action did irreparable damage to their marriage. They soon divorced.

*****

Jake and Marcy were taking their children to visit the zoo. The kid's argument over a zoo animal soon got out of hand. The kids began screaming and hitting each other. As Marcy turned around putting her arm up, she accidentally hit Jake's arm causing the car to veer to the left slightly sideswiping another car.

Gary Tyson, the driver flew into uncontrolled anger. He slowed down and pulling to the right slammed into the back of Jake's car, causing him to spin out of control. Airbags in the car prevented all but minor injuries to Jake and Marcy. The three children in the back seat were another story. Two were killed on impact; the other would be a quadriplegic for life.

Tyson's heavily damaged car was found a quarter of a mile up the road by police on their way to the accident scene. Nobody was in the vehicle. After investigating the accident, two of the officers returned to Tyson's car. Although a rental car, Gary's information was located at Avis. Police arrived at the airport as Gary Tyson was attempting to leave. They immediately arrested him and charged him with vehicular manslaughter.

A jury found him guilty of aggravated assault and first-degree manslaughter. The judge, who had no sympathy for the man, sentenced Tyson to twenty-five years to life.

Kerry Maine was a seasoned Hollywood actress. She had always prided herself in her ability to remain calm when behind the wheel. There had been several examples of her preventing an otherwise serious accident by slowing down or moving over. Unfortunately, the law of averages caught up with her one night.

Returning to her home in Beverly Hills, she was run off the road by another car. Because the car had passed her and sideswiped her for no apparent purpose, she reasoned it had been done out of spite. Her anger flared as she raced the Porsche she was driving to the side of the car ahead of her that had caused damage to her car and almost killed her. She turned her car strongly to the right, causing the car to veer off the highway and down the canyon where it exploded into fire. She was convicted of second degree manslaughter and given ten years in jail.

It's no secret. A moment of anger can cause a lifetime of sorrow. In fits of rage, people do things that can cause irreparable damage to themselves and others. There are many anger management classes throughout the country. Most of these involve teaching people to take a few minutes of heavy breathing in order to put a stop to it. Judges in minor cases, often give the defendant a choice between jail time and taking one of these courses. It can be an invaluable tool.

Chapter 14

A religion, practiced mostly in Haitian communities is voodoo. Voodooist's believe Bondye, meaning good God, is unreachable through prayer. They have to go through spirits called Loa. The practice descended from parts of Africa, who spoke Kikongo and were, captured, enslaved and brought to the United States. Originating in the Caribbean, the practice was suppressed by the Christian people of the time. When slaves were captured and brought to the Americas, the term Congo was substituted. In Yoruba, Kikongo people worship it as well.

The practice of voodoo is believed to ensure death will prepare one for a better life. The people don't believe in idols, however candles can be found, along with pictures of loved ones, throughout their homes. Unfortunately, as with other religions, there are always those trying to improve on the practice of voodoo. These include the beheading of chickens and other animals.

Paulo is an offshoot of pure voodoo. Its followers believe it harnesses the spirit of the dead to achieve its ends. In other cases, some leaders twist the meanings of the religion to fit their own personal needs

One such leader was Kami Madrassa, a self-proclaimed high priest and psychopath. As with most fanatical leaders, he set himself up as a Loa, and could speak to God directly. He had a large following in Florida's Haitian community. As usual he wanted to gain power. He did this by teaching that his followers would be heard by God and that they would have the supreme afterlife.

He started the practice of beheading humans, who wouldn't follow him. Their heads wound up in the homes of the victims' families. The heads were painted in such a way as to scare the families to come back into the fold.

The people there did not like police interference in their day-to-day business, especially when it came to their religion. For this reason, people going to the police were often looked upon as rats and would be punished or even killed for this act.

Kami formed bonds with two of the stronger believers, forming what is known as a dark triad. With the help of these men, he was able to build elaborate underground devices which could be raised and lowered at will. These included skeletal remains as well as other religious symbols. All this was done to achieve his fanatical ends.

As in all cases of this sort, a few rotten apples spoil the whole barrel. After a time Madrassa was brought to justice. He tried to get out of it by claiming freedom of religious rights. He was summarily tried and convicted on several counts of first-degree murder, as well as trying to incite riots. Eight years later, still professing his religious rights, he died by lethal injection in Florida's state penitentiary.

As with most religiously zealous leaders, he had a large following which supported him. These were mostly uneducated people from Haiti and Africa, who had superstitions instilled in them from birth.

Claudius Rebecas stepped in and took Kami's place as the sect's leader. He was not quite as ruthless as Kami, but very much a businessman. He convinced the followers that Kami had been unjustly prosecuted and that God chose to do nothing about it. Instead God proclaimed Claudius as their new Almighty Priest.

Having witnessed magical powers on the part of him and Kami, they blindly followed him. His proclamations over the next few years made him a very wealthy man. He is still in Florida somewhere running the lives of his flock, being careful not to go afoul of the law.

Chapter 15

A psychopathic behavior and form of hero worship is the drowning and then reviving of a person. It is most common in men in their teens and 20s.

James Boudreau was a classic example of this. Being a loner all his life, he began the practice shortly after getting out of high school. Most of his fellow students looked down on him as being "weird". The few girls he tried to talk to, seldom responded, and often turned away.

As a child he had been in one foster home after another. He was a bit of a troublemaker at that time. His parents, both drug addicts, had little time for him. The state of California had removed him from his parent's home and put him under foster care.

His first was at age 7. Mrs. Cowie tried to love the boy, with little success. Her husband, Bill, tried getting the boy interested in outdoor activities and even took him and the other boys in their care, camping on occasion. This was an exceptionally fine home for foster care.

They had four other children they cared for. Bill and his wife Mildred wanted to adopt James. As he began demanding more and more of their time, they decided against that. James began getting into fights with the other children. It was a hard decision, but after two years, Bill decided James had to go.

Three other homes followed. None gave James the care he was getting in the first. All three had other children they cared for and put up with James until he began hurting the other kids.

At age 14, James decided he'd had enough. He crawled out a window one night, and disappeared. His foster parents didn't mention this to the state and continued to collect money until they were caught. The state closed down their business.

Although the state had made a halfhearted attempt to find him, James had escaped into the woods several miles away. He found shelter in a cave and bounced between that and a nearby cabin, seldom used by its owners. He managed to find menial jobs in the area. Most of these jobs involved cutting back brush from homes for fire breaks.

He became more despondent as he realized he would probably never amount to much. His life changed one Saturday morning when he pulled a drowning boy from a nearby lake. The accolades given him by the parents of the boy, as well as other campers in the area, gave him a real boost to his self-esteem.

He found himself sitting on a boat dock on that lake more and more of the time. Realizing his actions were probably a once-in-a-lifetime shot, he began taking matters into his own hands. As there were several small lakes in the area, he was not tied to just one.

His first victim was a fourteen-year-old boy. James stunned the boy with a rock, and pulled him down to the lake. He threw the boy in the water, holding his head under for three minutes. He then pulled him out and onto the dock. His next move was trying to resuscitate the boy with chest compressions. When that didn't work, he tried mouth-to-mouth resuscitation. Realizing the boy was dead, James threw him into the lake. His body was found a couple days later, even though James had put him under a tree branch that was below the water as well.

Police ruled it as an accidental drowning, as water was found in the boys lungs. Although they saw the mark from the rock on the back of his head they figured he must've hit the bottom of the pier coming up out of the water. James decided this was no time to try it again.

After a couple of weeks, he felt a compulsive need to attempt it once more. Being the middle of summer, there were a lot of families camping around the lake areas. He had many people to choose from. He decided on a lake a couple miles from the first site.

Riding his bike to a camping area, he lay in wait for his next victim. Brenda Acuna was a young girl in her early teens. She was there with an older brother and his wife. Several hundred feet from their campsite was the water's edge. Her brother and sister-in-law had taken off to a near-by store, to get supplies.

This was a golden opportunity, if ever there was one. With nobody else close by, James was able to stun the girl and carry her to the lake. As she started to come to, he threw her in the lake holding her head underwater for a few minutes. Again, he pulled her out. The girl was gasping for air, so he pushed her under again. When he pulled her up, she had stopped breathing.

He brought her up a few feet from the shore, trying chest compressions once again. When that didn't revive her, he began to panic. Although this lake was in the same area as the first, it was in a different county. James counted on this as he threw the young girl's body back into the lake.

As time went on, authorities began to notice a rise in drowning's and put up danger signs around the lakes. James began burying his victims rather than throwing them back into the water. He had still not learned the fine art of reviving his victims, and soon realized he got just as much pleasure from drowning them.

Police were baffled as they now felt they my have a serial killer on their hands. Several people, mostly kids ages 10 to 20 were the victims. Police had not linked the drowning victims with those that had gone missing. All the lakes in the area were constantly being dragged for victims.

James became more and more arrogant and began getting sloppy. A couple of campers on a nature hike, witnessed James pulling a body out of the lake and heading up into the woods. They immediately called the police, who got to the burial site as James was throwing the last shovel of dirt on the makeshift grave.

He was tried and sentenced to death. However, when the state dropped the death penalty his sentence was commuted to life in prison without the possibility of parole.

Crimes of this sort are infrequent, but they are out there. The need to be a hero may, in few cases, drive young men into law enforcement as well as fire departments or paramedics. For the most part they are "type A" personalities. Most of us have had fantasies about saving the fair maiden in distress, but few ever get that chance.

Chapter 16

Another compulsion is hoarding. This is fairly common up to a point. However some people take it to the extreme where it becomes an obsessive-compulsive behavior.

This form of behavior was much more common in earlier generations, especially those that had gone through the Great Depression of the late 1920s. This type of hoarding can be as common as saving Christmas cards, and/or birthday cards.

Some more aggressive forms of this may include newspapers, magazines and books that will never be read more than once. Medications and foodstuffs that have gone way beyond their expiration dates are also good examples.

The police were called to an apartment building where the dead body of Lawrence Carson was found. When neighbors began to notice the smell, they notified the buildings managers. They in turn called the police. Officers had to break into the apartment, even though they had a key. Junk found in front of the door made it difficult to get through.

They were told Mr. Carson was a recluse and had needed supplies sent to him rather than going out. Police detectives surmised he was also Agoraphobic. Bags of canned goods as well as boxes of cereals and baking mixes were found cramming counter spaces and floor areas of the kitchen. So much stuff was pushed onto the floor that access to the kitchen, oven and refrigerator were practically non-existent.

Various types of rubbish, including worn-out furniture, clothes, shoes and other personal articles were found in both bedrooms. The bathroom didn't escape his treatment either. Police found medications, years beyond their expiration date, empty medicine bottles, piles of towels and wash cloths that hadn't been washed or used in decades. A path to the toilet and shower made up all the floor area in the room.

Besides that found on the floors and beds, they found clothes so tightly pushed together on hangers in the closet, it was practically impossible to pull anything out. Shoeboxes crammed the shelves as well as all sorts of paraphernalia. It is said, one fellow's crazy, is another's brilliance.

Being impossible to get his body to the front door, cleanup crews were called in to remove the junk. They say, "One man's junk is another's treasure". In this case Mr. Carson must've considered himself a very rich man.

*****

Another extreme example of this type of obsessive-compulsive behavior was found in a large multistory apartment building in La Mesa. This is a suburb of San Diego, California. What caused this man's behavior is hard to imagine. Being a high ranking general in the United States Army, he had the wherewithal to feed his addiction.

I saw this firsthand, being one of the people involved in the repair crews, working for Dunkel Construction Company, contracted by the building's insurance company. When I was told what happened, I honestly believed somebody was pulling my leg, hard.

This decorated military man, believed he was being watched by alien forces from another planet. He had covered all Windows and doors with aluminum foil. Although this has been seen in many cases, what came next was sheer insanity.

It must've happened over a period of years. He had drilled holes at the top of all the outside walls of the apartment, filling them, believe it or not, with M&Ms and other chocolate candies. Even buying them at the PX, the sheer cost of this must've been gigantic. A good part of the space in our two ton dump truck was filled with trash bags full of these.

His obsession was discovered after one of the downstairs neighbors called in a problem with his stoves range hood. Chocolate had been oozing down on top of it and onto the range.

Because of his military stature, rather than getting authorities involved, the man was evicted. He moved to an apartment somewhere in the Los Angeles area.

Who knows? Maybe over the last thirty years, and with a hell of a pension check, he may be up there, doing it again.

Marceline Garrett was a woman in her 70s. She, like many hoarders, seldom left her single bedroom home. The few friends she had, began to get worried when she hadn't shown up at the coffee clutch in a neighbor's home. One of the other women in the group offered to stop by her house on the way home. Knowing Marcy was a hoarder she knew she would be unable to see through the windows as they would be covered with all sorts of stuff. As she could not arouse her friend with the doorbell or loud knocking, Mimi called authorities. The fire department and ambulance, as well as police were there within a couple of minutes. After finally being able to get through the door they found Marcy dead on the floor from a stroke. They could tell she tried to get to the phone, but couldn't because of the junk on the desk.

Chapter 17

Although rare, another obsession is that of pulling out one's hair. This is known as Trichotillomania. It's rare, but it's out there. In most cases, it starts from infancy. This practice will often peak by the teen years. Most psychologists believe the practice starts as a habit and grows as a child gets older. Reasons given most frequently include satisfaction and even pleasure.

Victor Patterson was a young man of twenty-three years of age. He had found himself in a constant state of depression because of this habit. During his school years, and college, he was embarrassed by his compulsion, and resorted to buying a wig to cover it up.

In infancy, his parents began to notice this, as his playpen contained a lot of his hair. As in most cases of infants, this was done entirely on the scalp. His parents looked up a psychologist, who told them Victor would grow out of it. He never did, much to his parent's dismay.

Low self-esteem and embarrassment caused him to stay home-bound most of the time. Like most people with this condition, he had no intention of shaving his head. It took a couple of years with medication and psychiatric care to pull him out of the habit. He was one of the lucky ones; some people never recover from the condition.

By an 8 to 1 average, women are much more prone to this condition. Madeline Baker had suffered with it from her early teens. Now a young woman of twenty-four, she constantly tried to improve her appearance. For a reason, hard to understand, she began the practice at age 13. Her compulsion worsened as she got older, causing her much anxiety. She claimed, she didn't get any particular pleasure from this, but did it in an attempt to make her more desirable to men.

After marrying, her condition continued until her early 30s. A divorce and low self-esteem drove her to professional help. Today she is again happily married with two children. Although finding herself subconsciously pulling hair, when she thinks about it, she stops.

*****

Francis Lee had a rarer form of the condition. She not only pulled hair from her scalp, but from under her arms and pubic area as well. This caused her many problems. Thinking she was a complete freak of nature, she had severe bouts of depression and anxiety. Getting into a support group, which included several women with similar problems, she was able to get her condition under manageable control.

These are just a few examples of this compulsive behavior. Due to ones reluctance to admit a problem, caregivers feel there are thousands more out there, that don't seek professional help. This condition is probably more common than many think.

Claude Dixon had picked up the habit of pulling his hair when he was still in the crib. His parents thought little of it thinking he would grow out of it in time. When the habit continued into his early teens, his parents began to realize this was more than just a habit. They took Claude to a psychiatrist who diagnosed Claude with trichotillomania. He explained to Claude's parents that this was a fifty dollar word for habitually pulling one's hair. He took on Claude as a patient and after a year was able to curb the habit.

Claude has bouts of this obsession when under stress which is becoming more frequent as demands of his job increases. He has had to return to Doctor Gilmore on a few occasions to reinforce his mindset against this compulsion. His wife has been very understanding of his condition and realizes it's wise not to say anything when this habit takes over. Aside from this compulsion, Claude leads a very normal life with a loving wife and family.

Chapter 18

Love between gay couples is hard for straight couples to understand. Sometimes it's in the genetic makeup of people, but more often comes after birth. Some men can see the reasoning behind lesbian relationships, but not between two men. Women, on the other hand, can sometimes understand two men. In this chapter the study will center on psychotic behavior in some of them.

Felix Boxwood knew from a very early age that something was wrong with him. At that time being gay was looked on as a problem, not to be mentioned. His parents noticed all of his friends were male from the time he was a child. Going into puberty he found he didn't think the way other students did at school. He didn't consider it wrong never to ask girls out, however some of the other students did.

These problems got serious enough that his parents had to move him to another school. He was careful about what he said to other students. It was at the end of his last year of high school that he met Wiley. They became good friends, and pretty soon were inseparable.

The relationship became sexual after a couple of months. They managed to keep this bond between themselves. All that changed on a cold September night, when Felix took an unexpected trip to Wiley's apartment. Wiley was not the faithful partner Felix assumed he was. He had been seeing other guys as well. Laurence was one of these liaisons.

Coming in, seeing the two on the bed together naked, Felix became outraged. Picking up a nearby lamp, he killed both the young men. He tried to run, but didn't get far. Neighbors, knowing of his relationship with Wiley, told police. They put out an APB and Felix was soon apprehended. His attorney argued temporary insanity. Felix had an understanding judge and was charged with two counts of second-degree murder and sentenced to fifteen years in the state prison.

*****

Lonnie and Loretta were assigned the same room in the dormitory at the University of Iowa. Both girls were type A and had a high grade point average of 3.75. As time went on the girls kept talking to each other about the guys they were going out with. One night after a couple glasses of wine, without saying anything the two girls laid on the bed together. It started out innocently enough with a kiss on the cheek. Pretty soon their mouths were locked together, tongues darting in and out of both girls.

As the wine started doing its job on the girls, they stripped each other naked. Performing oral sex, both felt sensations the guys could never seem to give them. Afterwards they were perspiring and both were suffering from guilt trips. They crawled into their separate beds and fell asleep. The next morning neither of the girls said much of anything as they got ready for classes.

That evening getting back, both girls began studying. Afterwards the television came on, and as luck would have it, so did a romantic movie. It wasn't long before they were curled up together on the couch. They soon began a discussion of the night before. Before the movie was over, they turned off the television set and went to bed together.

Some of her closer friends soon learned of the relationship between the two. Roxy, who was herself a lesbian, began coming onto her best friend, Loretta. They tried to keep this relationship between themselves, but it wasn't long before Lonnie, feeling something was wrong, asked Loretta about it. She admitted to her other activities.

In a fit of rage, Lonnie stabbed her in the chest and genitals twenty-seven times. She was still sitting on the bed in tears as campus police got to their dorm. They were called by neighbors because of screams they were hearing. Lonnie was taken to the downtown jail where female detectives interrogated her for the next hour. Lonnie had snapped before police had gotten to her dorm. It was ruled that she was unfit to stand trial, and put into a state mental hospital before more appropriate action could be taken.

*****

Stephen and Tom were longtime partners, having been together almost 10 years. As time went on Stephen noticed a drop in Tom's attention span to him. When asked about this Tom admitted to having an affair with one of his co-workers. As Stephen had always been one hundred percent loyal to Tom, he flew into a rage. Tom had never seen him like this, and ran from their apartment. He got into his car and left.

Stephen followed him out the door, got in his car and tailed Tom to the freeway. Their speeds were reaching 90 miles an hour when Stephen rear-ended Tom's car, sending him reeling off the freeway and over a cliff. A woman entering the freeway from an on-ramp witnessed the incident and called 911. She waited for the police and gave them a clear description of Steven's car.

Although she was unable to get the make and model of the car, or a license number, she told police it was blue with a white top. The priority in most murder cases is to send police to the home of the victim to question the immediate family. On getting to the apartment building, they noticed a blue car with white top parked in the space for Tom's apartment.

They went to the door and knocked. Not getting an answer, they broke down the door. There was an empty whiskey bottle on the coffee table, and Steven's body lying on the floor. An ambulance was called, but he was pronounced dead at the scene. After an autopsy, his death was ruled suicide.

It's rare, but in some cases the wronged partner will commit suicide where they're sure their partner will find them. Coming home one evening Josh found Kenneth in the bathtub, both wrists slit. There was no suicide note, which Ken purposely did not write. He figured he'd get his pound of flesh with the law.

Unfortunately for Josh, he picked up the knife, getting fingerprints on it, besides blood on his arms and clothes. He wasn't thinking about that when he called 911. The police came, and after a few minutes took Stephen downtown for questioning. After five hours in an interrogation room, Stephen did not break. In his wallet was a time stamped ticket on the expressway. He hadn't thought about this until the end of his interrogation. The ticket proved he was innocent.

Stephen was set free. The coroner's jury ruled Kenneth's death a suicide.

*****

The town of Andrews Ville, South Carolina, was not the greatest place to hold a gay liberation parade. Rednecks abounded throughout the area. Police officers, many of who were in agreement with the rednecks, still had to protect the gay citizens as well. Police barricades had the main street roped off as men in costumes in all sorts of undress came down the street.

Although worried, the police thought they had a handle on the situation. About halfway through the festivities, gunfire rang out from one of the higher buildings. In the confusion, nobody saw where the gunfire was coming from. That would later be determined by the FBI, but in the meantime the perpetrator s escaped. Ballistics tests showed at least four guns.

Eighteen men were sent to the hospital with gunshot wounds. Six of them died in route. Three more were paralyzed from the waist down when shells went through their spine. It was a horrific day.

Nobody saw or knew anything, until the FBI put up a hundred thousand dollar reward for their capture. That was a little more than their "friends" could turn down. The four were caught within a week and sentenced to first-degree murder. In exchange for their admission of guilt, they were given life in prison without parole. Unfortunately, in that prison they were hailed as heroes by the other inmates.

Bobbi Ryan knew she was different from the other girls in her classes from the time she was a preteen. Unlike her friends, she seemed to have much more of an obsession with girls than with the boys. She constantly imagined being naked on a bed with other girls in her classes. She knew this wasn't normal, but she couldn't help herself. Boys just didn't interest her at all.

At age 13 she and her friend, Ruth began going to her home when her parents weren't there. They began playing with each other, rubbing each other on the buttocks and genitals as well as their developing breasts. They seem to enjoy each other more every time they got together. They were married in an offbeat church service, held on a local beach, at age 19, and witnessed by many of their friends. This wedding was against the wishes of both sets of their parents. This relationship lasted throughout their lifetimes.

Chapter 19

A condition known as body dysmorphic disorder is a condition in men and women alike. A person suffering from this is never pretty or handsome enough. Many of us may be unhappy with our appearance, but don't carry it to an extreme.

This condition is often found in entertainers. Many Hollywood actors and actresses have had so many facelifts and complete body makeovers they barely recognize themselves. This is understandable as there is a lot of competition for their jobs, especially those not in the limelight.

This disorder is not limited to those in the entertainment field. Many women feel if they don't keep themselves attractive, their husbands and friends may move on to greener pastures. In men, many have legitimate business reasons. This is especially true as they begin to age with grey hair and wrinkles. They realize the potential for younger women taking their jobs.

Madeleine Roche changed her name to Barbie O'Shea and moved to Hollywood California, where she took serious acting lessons. Her ambition, like most, was to become a famous star in the movies. With money she had inherited from her father, she found a good plastic surgeon and began changing her features as her monthly installments, from her father's attorney, came to her.

Over a period of a few months she had spent in excess of twenty-five thousand dollars. This money spent on facelifts, hair style and color changes, fatty tissue removal, breast enhancements, and clothes. Although an attractive woman in good physical condition she didn't see that. No matter what she did to improve her looks, in her mind, it was never enough.

Barbie achieved fame and fortune through working in soap operas over the next couple of years. She tried out, and began getting bit parts in films. Unfortunately, because of her success in soap operas she had become so recognized for them, producers were afraid to give her starring roles in films.

Having a compulsive desire to make it big drove her back to the plastic surgeons. This time she had smaller implants placed into her breasts, radically different hairstyles, colored contact lenses to change her eye color, and facelifts. So many changes had taken place, she barely recognized herself.

After the scars healed, she returned to the film studios. As a result of the changes she had made to her appearance, she finally achieved stardom. She had always been good at memorizing lines, seldom using the Teleprompter and knew enough to throw herself into the part she was portraying.

Over the next couple of years her fame and fortune grew. She was nominated for best actress in one of the films that had taken a sweep. Later she began to notice the parts she was given, were suitable for older women. This did not please her. Her surgeons had told her this may happen. At age 40 she started playing roles for grandmothers. She returned to the doctors that had performed her surgeries and was told that anything done at that point would be detrimental.

Having enough money and a beautiful home with a theatre, she retired and became a recluse, spending her time watching earlier soaps and movies she had starred in. She had forgone the pleasures of marriage and family. By age 60, she looked to be in her 80s. Had she really achieved what she wanted? Maybe, who knows?

Brad Walcott had gone through acting classes at UCLA and had become proficient in the art of acting. At age 25 he was handsome and with his acting abilities did very well for himself in films.

Striving to become the proverbial movie star, he began having enhancements on his face and body alike. A gym membership began getting him into good shape physically. Mentally, well, that was a different story. No matter what he did, which included facelifts, implants, hair styles and the like, he was never satisfied.

He was constantly growing beards, mutton-chops and mustaches, then shaving them off. This began to be a problem as his appearance could change many times in the course of the series he was starring in. He had been warned about this, the directors told him he'd have to put a stop to it. His obsession with this finally came to a head when his character was replaced by another actor.

These obsessive compulsions are not limited to the acting profession. Business professionals, people in the medical field, salesman, practically anybody meeting the public on a day-to-day basis can be affected by this. Women are much more prone to this than their male counterparts.

We all want to look our best, especially when dating or meeting new people. It's human nature. There are exceptions of course.

*****

William Millbrae was at the opposite end of that spectrum. Having his body tattooed from head to foot over a period of a couple of years, seldom bathing, cutting his hair and growing a beard, and just about anything else to make him look different from the clean-cut young man he had been. He was not in a biker gang or anything like that. However, he spent many of his evenings in the bars around San Francisco.

Portraying himself as a tough guy got him into trouble more than once. He worked in the computer field in Silicon Valley and made a decent living. Although intelligent, one would never have guessed it. He seemed to attract women in droves. He always treated them with respect, not the trait many of these girls were after.

One of these women managed to straighten him out. He was not able to get rid of the tattoos; however his compulsion to look like a slob soon changed. He is now enjoying his wife and family and just moved into an upscale home on Beacon Hill.

Dysmorphic disorder is instilled in many people, in varying degrees. Most of us never allow it to get to the point of being obsessive. It's in our nature to look the best we can with what we have. When it becomes a compulsion, it also becomes a problem.

Chapter 20

Luda-mania is the seldom used classification for people with a gambling addiction. Between 2 and 3% of the population admit to this addiction beyond the point of not being able to stop, once they start. Even after losing on any given day, the person or persons will often return to the casino, being certain they'll make up their losses.

Norma Jean Schafer had a gambling problem that started innocently enough. At the age of fourteen, she became a fourth at a table in her grandmother's home. They played straight draw poker for small amounts of money. In order to get her to enjoy herself, her grandmother innocently began to let her win.

Within a short time, Norma felt she really had a system for winning. By the age of eighteen she had become quite good at it. Although the adults no longer extended her the courtesy of winning, she began to do pretty well on her own. All this set her up for an addiction, almost impossible to conquer.

Gambling is considered by most psychologists to be the hardest of all compulsions to conquer. It is now looked upon by many as a disease, rather than an addiction. Luck cannot be manufactured, except for cheating, of course. The cameras situated in casinos do not allow for that. Gambling systems, by anybody that knows gambling, are considered pure insanity. To beat the house , many have tried attempts at just about everything from counting cards to palming them. However, multi-billion-dollar casinos are not built by giving the sucker an even break. Most casinos operate on a 2 to 3% profit margin overall.

Norma Jean began to gamble at one of the large casinos in Atlantic City. A bit of a winning streak in craps gave her confidence for bigger and better things. Two hours in that casino, increased her net worth by almost two thousand dollars. To her this was a lot of money. She figured a few more days like that would take care of her future education.

After a few more good days like that, between wins and losses, her bank account increased to almost twelve thousand dollars. She was given a free room at the casino and a five thousand dollar credit line. It didn't take long before she was dipping into that credit line.

She was soon into the casino for almost three thousand dollars. She was offered, and took a job, on the gaming floor as a waitress, and later as a receptionist in one of the cages. While on the job she began to notice that a lot of the big winners were soon big losers. Some people could come in and drop several hundred thousand dollars and not think anything of it. The majority of people could not. Many were gambling with welfare checks and rent money. A casino in San Diego County was once the largest casher of county welfare checks. Officials soon put a stop to that. Most of us can resist practically anything, but temptation.

Unlike most gamblers, Norma Jean realized she would never regain her losses. Within the month she was able to clear off her debt with the casino. Norma Jean started a support group for gamblers.

Although most gamblers will never admit to a problem, several do. Contrary to common belief, heads of casinos do not like to see people going into bankruptcy because of gambling, especially in their own houses.

One of Norma Jean's first members was Peter Austin. Peter had gone to Las Vegas where he developed a habit of watching high rollers make lots of money at the tables. He paid little attention when they were losing. He was soon a gambling addict himself. Having lost a good deal of money, he decided to move on. A bus ticket took him to Atlantic City, where he thought for sure he'd have better luck. Like Norma Jean he was given a line of credit, after a few wins and losses.

His wins and losses stayed pretty even for a couple of weeks. One lesson gamblers like Peter never learn is to quit while you're ahead. It's not hard to understand. When you're making money and having good luck you want to keep going. On the other hand when you're losing, you need to make back what you've lost. In Peter's case that was pretty much everything he had.

He secured a job with a construction company there, and soon made enough to get a small apartment. As soon as his bank account began to build, he was back at the casino trying to get it to build faster in the only easy way he knew. Soon his payroll checks were all flying into the casino's bank account.

With Norma Jean's help and that of some of the others in the group, he was able to curb his addiction to gambling. He realized, for the first time, he had a real problem that had to be addressed. Without the casino's help over the next year, he was able to get back on his feet.

Ron Johnson went to Las Vegas dreaming of making fortunes. This came from watching Texas hold 'em tournaments on television. He had learned a lot about the game from watching these programs. He realized he would have to be diligent about knowing when to call, or when to quit.

He began getting into the game and winning more often than he lost. Once in a while he would get careless, but for the most part he did pretty well. He was one of the lucky ones and realized this game was becoming a compulsion. Being several thousand dollars ahead, he took his winnings back to his home in Tucson Arizona.

Ron was one of the select groups that knew to quit when he was ahead. Although he'll take a trip to Las Vegas on occasion, he never takes more money than he can afford to lose. He has a good job, but he also has a family to support. He has no intention of jeopardizing that.

William Burton, unlike Ron, never knew when to quit. His jackpots were never big enough to offset his betting. Ron did his gambling at the racetrack. In lieu of this he would do track betting at the casino in his town. He used every trick in the book to pick the right horses. He could often be seen in the stables looking at the horses and talking to their owners. He would sometimes make bets on the names given these animals, or the position of the moon the night before. Nothing was too far out to convince him he was making the right bet. Thankfully Ron was reasonably wealthy. He had been left stock by his mother, upon her death. He never realized this inheritance wouldn't last forever.

Ron can now be seen cleaning out the stables at the racetracks. To his credit he has finally learned his lesson and no longer bets on the ponies.

Lotteries have become a huge cash cow for many states. The California lottery had a direct impact on the Indian gaming casinos. In San Diego, a large casino had been raided by police. At one time, bingo was about the only legal form of gambling with the exception of card rooms. Being on Indian land, the casino put in slot machines. My brother happened to be in this casino the morning it was raided by authorities, claiming they were immoral. They began removing the machines.

When the casino offered to give the state a percentage of the winnings, the machines were returned to the floor the next day. The State Supreme Court judged the slot machines to be legal declaring the state lottery was a form of gambling. Therefore the casinos were off the hook.

The compulsion for gambling has ruined many people, both men and women and especially families. A lot of people have been wiped out thinking they could beat the odds. Some do but most do not. The ones that are lucky usually wind up back in the casinos. Gambling is a hard compulsion to break, however because of the efforts of organizations like gamblers anonymous, it can be done.

Chapter 21

One obsession found mostly in people in their teens and early 20s is called phoba-ado. In these cases siblings fall in love with each other. In most cases they are children that have been orphaned. For mutual protection they choose to live together.

This attraction, over a period of time, may become sexual in nature. Back in the dawn of our history this practice was considered normal because of the lack of suitable mates. Of course today it's considered immoral and illegal.

Joshua and Fanny Jones were brother and sister. Their parents were killed in an automobile accident and they were left in the care of the state.

Orphaned at age 12 and 16, neither had social skills. They depended on each other to sustain themselves. This was soon carried into the bedroom as well. They fell in love with each other. Knowing they could not marry legally, they decided to live together.

After a couple of years, Fanny became pregnant and gave birth to an autistic child. The boy also showed signs of cerebral palsy. He became too much to care for, and his parents put him in a state run institution.

Because of this Joshua had himself sterilized with a vasectomy. They lived together their entire lifetime, neither becoming attracted to anyone else.

*****

Bert and Janice were first cousins. At an early age, they played together. As time went on, their games became more serious. In their early teens they became sexually active with each other. Bert was careful to use protection so as not to get Jan pregnant. They managed to keep their parents in the dark over this attraction.

After both graduated from the University of Washington, Bert took a job on the other side of the country, and Janice followed. They also lost contact with their families. They drifted apart over the next couple of years, and by mutual agreement begin to date outside their relationship. Soon, both were married and had families. Although attracted to each other, they managed to keep their mutual attraction in check.

This fascination is not as unusual as one may think. The relationship is usually kept in the closet. In most cases, after the physical attraction wears off, both will go on to lead normal lives. However in other cases one of the partners may not, and will remain attracted to the other.

Chapter 22

Dissociative personality disorder, better known as split personality is a mental condition in which a person's personality is altered from one state of thought to another. It is one of the most controversial of all psychiatric conditions. It's generally accompanied by memory impairment, going beyond normal forgetfulness. In some instances, extreme trauma has been known to cause this. Cases have been tried in court, and have met with some degree of success, but not much.

Tony Summers was a man in his late 20s. He was a slight man and not temperamental in any way. Late one evening, several years before, he was attacked in the New York subway by two young men. They stuck the barrel of a gun hard against his head, enough to cause pain and trauma.

When taken into custody, Tony didn't know what had happened to him. When the train pulled into the next station, Tony was sitting on the seat next to two dead gunmen. He had no idea how the gun got in his hand. He was immediately arrested and tried for first-degree murder.

Because of an exemplary police record, and the fact that both of the young men had long records of rape and robbery, Tony's case was being given a hard look. He claimed he had no memory of what happened after the gun went to his head. Doctors found the area of his head where he had been hit. It did not result in a concussion, however the wound was noticeable.

Tony was tried and convicted of second degree manslaughter, and sentenced to fifteen years in prison, with the possibility of parole in ten. This was due to the records of the young gunmen. Tony was sent to the state prison in Attica New York.

Being slight in build, he became an easy target for some of the inmates. It began with a few catcalls in the shower, within a couple of months it became a serious problem. One morning when the guards were making their rounds, they found a dead body lying on the floor of Tony's cell. How he got in the cell was a good question.

The man had his pants around his knees and lay in a pool of blood. It was found, the keys came from one of the guards who was given money for the use of the key for a half hour. He was immediately dismissed from the prison system and prosecuted.

Angelo Barra was a lifer. He was known around the prison as a bully. This was far from being the first time he had tried to commit acts of sodomy on other, weaker prisoners. Tony was found scrunched up on the bed, shaking. He was questioned intensively on what had happened. He had no memory of the incident. One of the prisoners in another cell, Frank Sutter, came forward when asked if he saw anything. He and Tony hadn't really become friends; however they did speak to each other at the cafeteria on occasion.

The warden, who had questioned Tony earlier, came into the room where they had taken Frank Sutter. The people sitting in the room could scarcely believe what they were hearing.

Tony began begging the man to leave him alone, to the point of crying softly. Angelo laughed, and Tony quit crying. He went into a flying rage and beat the man to death. When Sutter asked Tony what happened, he said his name wasn't Tony. The warden felt this had to be looked into further. He had read the transcripts from Tony's trial, and thought it was a ruse to get off. Now he wasn't so sure.

Tony was transported by ambulance, to a psychiatric hospital. There he was giving a battery of tests trying to determine what was wrong with him. During electric shock treatments, his alter ego appeared. He was almost able to break free of his restraints. The two guards as well as the doctor looked on in disbelief.

Most of the split personality cases Dr. Morris had been called on to look into had turned out to be fabrications. After getting "Harry" to calm down, he went back to being Tony. Because of these results Dr. Morris had Tony transferred to a psychiatric hospital. After several days of tests, he was given medications as well as therapies, to help keep him calm.

After a year he was paroled on the condition he stay on his medications, which were carefully monitored. Harry never reappeared throughout Tony's lifetime.

*****

Lily was a woman in her 20s. She was popular and well-liked by the other students at the University where she attended medical school. One night, at a popular nightspot in town, a couple of her friends had decided to party. They saw Lily sitting in the booth with two men. This was completely out of character for her. They walked over to the table to say hi to their friend. Lily acted as though she had never seen them, and had no idea what they were talking about.

She claimed her name was Wanda. Lily's two friends went over to the bar and ordered a couple of beers. "Wanda" paid no attention to them. The girls noticed her behavior to be odd indeed. They assumed that Wanda must be a twin sibling. On the way back to their dormitory, the girls decided to ask Lily about her the next day, as she had never mentioned having a sister.

The next morning they asked Lily about that. She said she didn't have a sister, and it was odd because they weren't the first ones to ask her that. They say everybody has a twin, and Lily and the girls assumed it was a case of mistaken identity. The subject was dropped and forgotten.

Wanda continued to exist until Lily's graduation. Strangely enough word got around campus that Lily and Wanda were not related to each other. Stranger still, Wanda was never seen returning to Lily's apartment. When she was spotted, the others assumed it was Lily.

A couple of years later, Lily began working as a nurse at the Memorial Hospital in town. A new patient being treated for associative disorder had been admitted to the hospital, and handcuffed. He was one of her patients. She became fascinated by this when he told her what had happened.

Gerald Markey had been aware of this problem most of his life. His parents first noticed it after having a Hollywood glass door fall on their son's head at age 6. He had always been a docile child and pretty much did what he was told. Another side of him came out a few months later.

At recess, one of the class bullies began picking on him at school. The teacher noticed an immediate change in his behavior as she was watching the class on the playground. He began beating on the kid that had bullied him. The boy required stitches.

Since that time, Gerald had a few episodes like this. His parents witnessed one for the first time when he was twelve years old. He was getting into puberty, and testosterone and rebellion followed. At first his parents assumed he was going through a stage.

One morning when his mother put her foot down and ordered Gerald to take out the trash, Gerald's alter ego came out. He blackened one of his mother's eyes and pulled her hair before his father, a police officer, was able to get into the kitchen and pull Gerald off of her. Not knowing what else to do, he restrained the kid on a chair in handcuffs. After he settled down, Gerald had no memory of what he had done to his mother. She was in the living room on the couch, crying.

When his father had explained to him what happened, he went into his mother in tears and apologized to her. She took him in her arms and forgave him. When Gerald took out the trash, his father sat down and explained to his wife what had happened. They both realized their child needed help. Here again the doctor prescribed medication for him, stopping the problem.

Lily became fascinated, as she listened to the young man recount the stories earlier in his life. He told her he had not had the problem again until a couple of days before, when his girlfriend was shot and killed in his apartment. The assailant didn't realize Gerald was in the other room. He literally threw the man out of the three-story window in her apartment. He ran downstairs, and was beating on the dead body when police got there. He was immediately restrained, arrested, and taken to jail.

After about an hour in jail, he was taken into an interrogation room and questioned. By that time, he calmed down and had no recollection of what he had done. He did explain to the detective that he had this disorder. This was confirmed when the detective called Gerald's parents. He was taken to the hospital.

Remembering the incident in the bar a couple years before, Lily began to wonder if that encounter at the bar may have been a problem with her.

She got her answer several months later, when one of the doctors invited her out for dinner and drinks. Unfortunately the drinks came first. Although this was her first attempt at a hard drink, she seemed to enjoy it. Unfortunately the long island iced tea she had ordered was not exactly what she expected. It was, in fact, the most powerful of all mixed drinks. The effect of the drink hit her before the dinner came.

Ordering her another drink, her date for the night, the doctor sitting across from her, noticed a dramatic change. She had no idea who Frankie or Lily was. She asked that he leave her table. He went to the waiter and asked that he bring her dinner to her table and his to a separate table nearby. He also asked that he refuse her any more drinks, except water. After a half hour, Frankie noticed Lily come back to reality. She looked at him strangely, wondering how and why he was sitting at the next table.

She could scarcely believe what she was hearing. This story was confirmed by the waiter when he came back with their dessert. Like Gerald, she was given a much milder form of the medication and told to stay away from hard liquor. It was not known whether table wine would have the same effect, but she never took that chance.

As a footnote to this case, Gerald was found guilty of justifiable homicide. After six weeks in the mental hospital, going through some therapy and medication adjustments, he was released.

*****

Not all cases of this disorder are Jekyll and Hyde. Leroy Carter had always been a problem child. At age 15, he robbed a gas station, shooting the owner in the head. He was not on drugs, and made sure there were no video cameras in the store before he held it up. Wearing gloves on his hands and booties on his feet, he was careful not to touch anything except the cash register, which he emptied, then wiped clean of fingerprints. Being the middle of the night and out in the middle of nowhere, he was not caught.

A couple of nights later a similar incident took place several miles away by Leroy's alter ego. Police were baffled by the similarities except for the fact the clerk had been stabbed several times in the chest. Figuring whoever did this would be covered with blood, they checked the dumpster outside. They assumed the attack was caused by a large man. They felt anybody going behind the clerk would've left bloody footprints on the floor. They hadn't counted on the booties, which went on after the attack.

Several more of these types of attacks went on undetected in other states throughout the country. FBI detectives were baffled as they knew they had a serial killer on their hands, but most serial killers stick to a script. The assumed there had to be two killers working together.

When Leroy was shot to death by an off-duty police officer in the back of a store, the FBI continued to look for his accomplice. They, nor anyone else, realized this man had associative personality disorder. The manhunt was discontinued after no new cases in a six-month period. The case went into a cold case file, and to this day, has never been taken out.

Bonnie Rodriguez had this condition, and was with the border patrol. The disorder never manifested itself until after she had gotten the job, just out of college. She had strong feelings for border security, as her father had been killed while chasing an illegal alien. She was still on probation one evening when a car drove through her window without stopping. She called ahead to have it stopped. The car returned and she began to inspect it. Two men attacked her when she opened the trunk. She went wild, killing them both. She came to in handcuffs hardly believing what she was hearing. She could remember none of it. Two of her fellow workers told her she'd addressed herself as Katie. She was taken to a mental hospital, and found to have the disorder.

Chapter 23

The next condition to be looked at is extremely dangerous. It's referred to as violent-schizoid personality disorder. It is a desire to kill man, or beast. This is done for no particular reason. The more common cause of this can be PTSD (post-traumatic stress disorder). This is most commonly found in those coming back from military service overseas.

....

Donald Sieverts was one such example. He came home after the first gulf war. Unfortunately, neither his parents nor anybody else noticed the change in his behavior. He was sullen most of the time, taking long walks to ease his anxiety. He felt a need to carry a knife, for his own protection.

On one of these walks, a dog came out of the yard and threatened him. As the dog made a lunge at him, he pulled the knife and killed the animal. He felt unusually calm, and ecstasy overcame him. Although during his service career, he had killed a few combatants, he had not gotten the thrill he was now experiencing.

His obsession was in animals for the next year. As the obsession grew so did his need. He began to look for human victims. Being not far from a college, he determined students would be easy prey.

Brian Kimball was walking across campus after a party one evening, when he felt the knife against his throat. That was the last experience he had.

Police detectives spent days looking for a motive. Brian's wallet and watch were untouched. His classmates were devastated. He was an honor student, well-liked and admired by those who knew him. Detectives could find no motive for his untimely death. Their only thought was that it may have been the work of a knife wielding, homeless man, killed by police the night before. They still couldn't figure out why he hadn't stolen Brian's wallet,

That explanation satisfied everyone involved until the following week when a female victim was found in the bushes on the college campus, stabbed in the chest. The coroner found she had not been sexually violated. This scared police, as they realized they probably had a serial killer in their midst.

Sieverts decided to expand his killing area into the next county. His first victim was an elderly gentleman out for a walk one night.

Gerald Westmoreland was a widower living in a nearby senior retirement home. These walks were a routine nightly exercise for him. Being in excellent condition for a man of his age, he felt taking these walks at night would prolong his health and longevity. Little did he know, just the opposite was true.

He was grabbed around the chest. He tried to explain to his attacker that he had no money. That did no good, as the knife pierced the carotid artery on the right side of his neck.

Police detectives reasoned the attacker was left-handed. Due to the upward cut on his throat they surmised he was probably a large male. The violence involved in this attack was not understood. Westmoreland had a reputation for being kind and gentle. His funeral services that weekend were attended by most of the people living in the retirement home.

Getting information from the neighboring Police Department, police knew they had a serial killer in their midst, as all three attacks had been basically the same, performed by a large, left-handed person. As they were aware of the military personnel coming back from the Mideast, they reasoned one of these people suffering from PTSD could be their serial killer.

These killings did not cross state lines. However, because of possible military involvement, the FBI was notified. The criteria of personnel that were large and left-handed, with a mental problem, were narrowed down to just a few. All had alibis on the nights of the murders. The exception was Donald Sieverts. Around-the-clock surveillance was instituted by the police and FBI. After a week these actions bore fruit. They followed Donald to an alley-way where, knife in hand, he grabbed a homeless man.

The Detectives called for backup and brought two radio cars to the location. Sieverts turned facing police with his knife to the man's throat. When he refused to put the knife down, police felt it necessary to take action. They shot Sieverts in the forehead, killing him instantly.

Not all of these killings have the military to blame. Most often, a broken home comes to the top of the list of reasons.

*****

One such example was 18 year old Adam Viceroy. He walked into a high school gymnasium with a gun. He wasn't trying to prove anything, as he had a bag over his head. All five of the students survived the attack, by no-fault of Adams. Some were shot up to three times.

None of those attacked had any idea who had done this. Adam was not satisfied. Although he had no axe to grind, he wanted them dead. He decided to kill them when they returned. He realized the only way this would work would be to get them all together in one spot. This was accomplished a couple weeks later, when the five got together in a park to celebrate their good luck in surviving the attack.

Unfortunately, as he had used a separate gun, the police were not closer to catching him, than they were before. The detectives were baffled as ballistics showed two different guns.

Adam had removed the guns from his grandfather's gun cabinet. His grandparents were taking a holiday cruise. On returning his grandfather noticed the gun cabinet had been jimmied. Adam claimed he found an unlocked side door open when he got home from class. This satisfied his grandfather, but not the police. Ballistics on the gun showed they both came from his grandfather's collection. They immediately took Adam into custody for questioning. After five hours of intensive interrogation, the kid finally broke. He admitted to the killings as well as four others. He was tried and sent to an institution for the criminally insane. Being tried as an adult, he would never get out.

*****

Although rare, some of these murders have been caused by women. Darlene Mason was well-liked in school, especially by the boys. She was brutally raped by Brad, her prom date. A couple of days later she got her revenge. Her rape had not been reported, so she felt safe taking the law into her own hands. Brad was shot to death on his front lawn.

Having had a taste of the violence in the shooting of Brad, she found sexual pleasure in the killing. This started a spree of murder. Her victims were both male and female. They ranged in age from 14 to 30. Police detectives had not been confronted with a female serial killer. As most of the killings had no rhyme or reason, police were baffled.

Several other killings took place in three different county areas, until one of her roommates reported that she had mysteriously disappeared the nights of the shootings. Police thought nothing of this at first, but seeing a gun on her bed one night, her roommates felt police should be notified.

She was taken into custody but demanded an attorney. Because of this she was arrested and booked on suspicion of nineteen counts of first-degree murder. Ballistics from three different guns, two of them under her mattress, proved her guilt. She was sentenced to death by lethal injection.

*****

Another strange case of this nature happened in a small town in the Midwest. Several men and women in the town of Burtonsville were coming up missing from their homes. This case had police baffled, until they began to realize that all these people were prominent members of the community. As this was happening on a weekly basis, state police were called in on the investigation.

Police and volunteers were being assigned to keep an eye on anybody in a prominent position in the town. This included business owners, people involved in the politics of running the town, and lifetime residents.

As of yet police could find no common denominator for the missing people. It made no sense to them that all of these disappearances could be voluntary. In all the cases, personal belongings, such as wallets and purses, which were not tampered with, were still in their homes. Family members were either out of the house, or sleeping upstairs when their loved ones became part of the list of missing persons.

As in many cases, hunter's dogs became the key to cracking the case. These dogs found a shallow grave in a wooded area about a mile from town. When the authorities arrived on the scene, the area had already been roped off by the hunters who had located the grave.

The first body was found 2 feet below the surface. Another body was found 2 feet below that. They both showed one gunshot to the forehead. When no other body was found at the gravesite, they widened the search finding twelve more bodies. The bodies were taken to the Medical Examiner's Office, in Burtonsville, for autopsy.

When the bodies were opened, medical examiners could find nothing out of place. This baffled them until opening their mouths. They found the tongues of all of these people had been cut out. The examiners were puzzled by this. Why the tongues?

Psychiatric personnel from the FBI were called in from a neighboring city. Because of the reputation a lot of people in politics, the examiners asked themselves if these people always had a reputation for being truthful.

In questioning friends and family, they found they had their common denominator. Knowing this, did not put them any closer to the perpetrator. The shells recovered from the bodies, some of which were almost unrecognizable, were taken to ballistics and shown to be fired from the same gun; a forty-four Magnum.

Gun permits were checked by the state police. The people in the town, having that caliber handgun checked out okay. Now the police were really puzzled. They widened their search to 100 mile radius and hit pay dirt in a small out of state town about 50 miles away. The gun had been registered under the name of Billy Stedman. He was known in town to be a bit of an oddball, but was never considered a threat to anybody. He lived alone just outside of town.

In his home, agents found what they were looking for in Billy's basement. Hidden under the bottom drawer of the dresser, was the gun they were looking for. In a jar, tucked away on a nearby shelf, investigators found a large cookie tin. On opening it, they found all the missing tongues. Police drove to the café where Billy worked as a dishwasher. He was taken into custody without incident.

Officers took him to jail, where he was questioned about their discovery. When he realized he would never get away, he gave them his explanation. He told them that he overheard conversations from the victims in the café, about what they were doing, and getting away with. He told police they were all damned liars, but they wouldn't lie to God. He was tried and put into a state mental institution for life.

Killings of this nature are the hardest to prove and have a low conviction rate because of it. Unless caught in the act, or evidence being found on their person or in their homes, police will try to keep them in custody until evidence can be found. Lack of appropriate evidence has been responsible for a few too many acquittals. The saying, "it's not what you claim, it's what you can prove", holds water.

Jason Teagan had just gotten out of high school when his killing spree began. None of his friends had any idea Jason would capable of hurting anybody. His first victim was an elderly woman getting off a bus in Long Beach California. It was late and dark when he attacked her.

Authorities could find no reason for the attack as she was a lifelong resident and had many friends. The police investigation that ensued came up dry. About a week later another senseless killing took place in nearby signal Hill. Again police could find no reason for the murder of a middle aged man. What caught the eye of the detectives was the similarity of the two murders. Both were carotid and stabbed in the heart. After a similar attack in Newport Beach, police knew they had a serial killer on their hands.

Jason was seen killing a man in a wheelchair at the park and police were notified. Unfortunately they didn't get there in time to save the victim, but stopped Jason as he was fleeing the scene. He was tried and convicted of first-degree murder and sentenced to life in a mental hospital in San Francisco. His reasons would never make sense, even if they were known.

Chapter 24

Some people have a compulsion to commit cold-blooded murder. In many cases of this type, sexual satisfaction is the motive. A rapist may kill his victim to escape prosecution. These cases vary from one type of personality to another. In some cases a man may be impotent and unable to obtain an erection without killing his victim.

In some instances, couples will commit murder for the same reason. In most cases the wife may be an unwilling participant. This was not the circumstance with Samuel and Victoria Bachman. In their case, they would lure a young man or woman to a hotel room, using a three-way sexual experience as an excuse. At that point Samuel would garrote the victim as soon as he or she was in front of him. This would be done slowly, usually with a rope and sometimes with a wire, depending on the size of the victim.

The victims were petite enough, mostly done with young women; Victoria would commit the murder on occasion. Afterwards, leaving the victim lying on the floor, the two would undress and have sex on the bed. Samuel had done this on his own, before meeting and falling in love with his wife. At that time he performed the act solo.

After this act had been committed, they would Stuff the body in a large suitcase, and take it out the front door of the hotel. The clerk would assume it was their luggage. They would then take the body to a local cemetery late at night, and bury it. They had killed twenty victims before being caught. It was by accident a passing off-duty police officer noticed the two behind the locked gates at a local cemetery, carrying a body. He pulled over to investigate. He called for backup, and arrested the two, on the spot, for suspicion of murder. Those suspicions were well-founded. The bodies were all recovered.

Samuel and Maria were sentenced to death in the electric chair. They were in prison for five years awaiting execution. On the night before her execution, Victoria was handcuffed and taken into the viewing room and watched her husband as he died. Prison officials felt this was justifiable. Serial killers tend to screw up when things get personal.

*****

Jeremiah Smith was a man of twenty-seven. He got a perverse thrill from watching somebody in the throes of death. This came from an earlier hunting trip when he was a teen. After shooting a deer in the woods, he walked up to claim its body. As he had missed vital organs, he watched in fascination as the buck died. He was sexually excited by this and relieved himself on the animal's body.

So great was the satisfaction that he began to imagine himself killing a human and watching the person die, as he masturbated. This behavior satisfied him for a while. This obsession became a reality and a compulsion. The strange thing was that it didn't matter whether the person was male or female. The thrill was the same with both.

The majority of his victims, which numbered twelve, he found sitting by themselves on a park bench. Coming up from behind he would stab his victim in the back. Being sure nobody was around, he would then put the person on the ground. After the act he buried the body in a shallow grave, off the beaten path. A jogger on a nearby trail caught him in the act one night and called police. He followed Jeremiah to the burial place, giving police directions.

Jeremiah was taken in and charged with twelve counts of first-degree murder. He made a plea agreement, through a legal aid attorney, for life in prison instead of execution, if he told them the whereabouts of the other eleven victims. This was done, and he is now in state prison with no possibility of parole.

*****

Diane Richter was a woman of twenty. In many cases involving women, having a stepfather molest them at an early age, or being raped at some time in their life, is usually what sets them off. Diane had no such excuse. She was physically fit and came from a loving home. She had no problems until high school. During that time she got involved in drugs, but kicked the habit after a couple of years in college. She stayed clean, but for some reason had a fascination with killing and death.

This fascination started after her college years. In the space of four years she had killed eight people. Three women and five men were shot to death for no apparent reason. Regardless of their size, she dragged her victims to the edge of a pier and threw them off. She didn't bother to weigh them down, so they were often found within a day or two.

Because of the brutality involved and the size of some of the victims, police had no idea their suspect was a woman. There was never evidence of sexual misconduct, which baffled the police as well. They suspected gangland hits.

As in most cases of this type, Diane got cocky and careless. A boat docked out, not far from the pier, sat with its lights out. Aboard the boat, a man and woman were sitting on the deck enjoying the warm evening. They witnessed one of the body dumps. Using binoculars, the man could clearly see it was a woman and gave the police sketch artist a good description.

Diane's picture was on the front page of the newspaper the next morning. She tried to escape town, but was caught in a police roadblock several miles from her home. She was tried and convicted of first-degree murder. The sentencing jury, felt she was sane at the time of the murders and sentenced her to life in the state prison, without parole.

*****

David Sawyer was a man of twenty-three. He had been in and out of jail since age 15. It was during imprisonment, that he got a taste of sodomy, both committing and receiving. Because of his age and build, he was often the victim. He was out of jail about four months when an overwhelming compulsion struck him. At first his partners were willing participants, but as time went on he started becoming more and more sadistic.

His first major thrill came when he accidentally killed his partner. This guy was into S&M, and asked David to beat him. Dave got carried away at this request, and beat the man to death. He lay in bed that afternoon, thinking about the experience he'd had.

He put the man through the window of his room under the cover of darkness. He then drove his car to the back of the motel and put the body in the trunk of his car. Having a blanket in the car he was careful not to get any blood or DNA sample in the car. He drove the body several miles out of town, and threw it into a ravine.

After a couple of weeks reliving that experience in his mind, over and over again, he made the decision to do it again. This time he had no willing partner. The young man was a street person who David offered to help, with a hot meal. After a dinner at the local diner, David asked the man to help him move a refrigerator out to his garage. The man was happy to oblige. David drove about 3 miles out of town in the opposite direction of where he had dumped his first victim.

Being a cabin on the property the young man thought nothing of getting out of the car and walking up to it. Before getting to the door, David hit the man with a rock stunning him and knocking him to the ground. He then strangled the man until he was no longer breathing. Afterwards he took the guy several hundred feet behind the cabin, and buried him in a shallow grave.

His next victim was nineteen-year-old Susan Davies, living in a college dorm. David was careful to find a girl that had no roommate or immediate family. Susan was a nice looking young girl who was kind of shy.

As she got off the bus one night and walked towards her room, David popped out from behind a bush and strangled her to death. The street was unlit, making it easy for David to carry the body to his car. He then drove his kill out of town where he buried her.

Surprisingly David held no more of a thrill with the young woman, than he had with the men. However at that point, he felt much safer with the weaker sex. University personnel began noticing their students going missing. As some of the first were during the holidays, they didn't think much of it, until the girls didn't return. At that point they got the police involved.

A major manhunt ensued, although police had little to go on. Warnings were put out around the college and an increased University and city police presence was instituted. Detectives staked out all bus stops near the buildings. The news media was kept in the dark about this, as police felt this policy was their best chance to catch the perpetrator.

A week later, David, unknowingly tried to take down an undercover female police officer. That was a big mistake on his part. Her training in the martial arts caused David a lot of pain before other officers got to the scene. He went to the hospital with a concussion and a broken nose.

He was able to make a deal with prosecutors to spare execution, if he revealed the location of the other bodies. There were thirteen in all. David would spend the rest of his natural life in *a cell at the state prison.*

*****

Susan Rand was a woman in her mid-20s. As a prostitute in a large city, she was used to being propositioned by men in hotel bars. Because of this, most of these men were transients. She began to accept these men's invitations for a night on the town. Afterwards on the way back to the hotel, these men were only too happy to pull off the road for a little pre-sex fun. This became a serious mistake on their part.

During the course of the evening, she would pull the derringer out of her bag, killing the man before he could stop her. She would then pull the man into a backwoods area where she dumped him. She pulled this on twenty victims before being caught.

A man, Coon hunting, came upon her one night as she was dragging her victim to his resting place. He followed her back to her car and was able to get a license number, which he turned over to the police. She was picked up and jailed. Her insanity plea fell on deaf ears. She was tried and convicted of twenty counts of first-degree murder and sent to death row.

*****

Spencer Kenwood was a serial killer for two years before he was finally caught. He would kill his victims on a night with a full moon. This probably had something to do with it. He made his kills in seventeen states. His twenty-seven victims, all men, were never sexually assaulted; however they were stripped naked after death. These kills had law enforcement convinced he was gay even though no sign of sexual activity was ever recorded. Police felt the person doing this was probably male due to the size of his victims. Having an accomplice was ruled out early on. Detectives felt, even using a condom, there would be some evidence of sexual misconduct.

Spence had a wife and two children. In all respects, he seemed to be a happily married man. His wife knew nothing of the other side of him. Being a salesman for a clothing manufacturer had him on the road, and in the air a good part of his time. Nobody caught on that these trips coincided with the moon. Being an amateur astronomer he had an obsession with phases of the moon. Why a full moon would act on his compulsion to kill, was not known. These kills being interstate resulted in the FBI getting involved.

They had several leads in various states, even of eyewitness sightings to these kills, however nothing was concrete. Nothing, that is until a woman took a picture of him during a murder. The FBI caught up with him a couple days later at his home.

His wife was in hysterics, as she saw her husband being led away in handcuffs and put into the back of the police vehicle. She was questioned and convinced police she knew nothing of her husband's activities.

•••

Spence was tried and convicted of first-degree murder in four of the cases. The death penalty was taken off the table providing he gave the FBI names of his other victims. He was sentenced to life in prison without the possibility of parole. A lack of evidence has been responsible for a few too many acquittals. The saying, "it's not what you claim, it's what you can prove", holds water. This was thankfully not the case with Spencer Kenwood.

Chapter 25

Patrick Moore thought he had good reason to kill, which he did not. He would fly into a fit of anger for no apparent reason. His imagination often ran wild with him. On one occasion he stopped by his supposed friend, Colleen's house. He had been infatuated with her for some time, and dated her a couple of times. Not seeing a car in her driveway, he drove on wondering why she wasn't there. He just knew she was out with another guy. He began getting mad and the more he thought about it the more incensed he got. He turned around and went back.

She was just getting back from a Pilate class. He attacked her on the front porch. Pushing her through the front door he proceeded to get a knife and stabbed her thirty-two times in the chest.

He then went to the home of his best friend, whom he thought was seeing Colleen. When Jack opened the door, Patrick pushed him back onto the floor. Jack was stabbed in the right eye, and seventeen times in the chest and abdomen. The sad part of this story was that Jack and Colleen barely knew each other.

Realizing what he had done, Patrick drove to his mother's apartment. He sat with her for a couple hours getting more agitated as the morning wore on. Television news was broadcasting the story of the two murderers. His mother realized Patrick knew both of these people, and asked him if he was involved. He swore to her he wasn't, but got in his truck and sped away.

He had a couple more people he wanted to see before he left town. One was a man Patrick was sure had gotten him fired, from the garage where he worked. Stopping there, he beat the man to death with a tire iron. His last victim was his mail carrier. He blamed the man for keeping Colleen's letters to himself.

Going by his house, Patrick ran the man down with his truck and sped away. He got onto a freeway where he was stopped by a highway patrolman for speeding. He argued with the officers telling them he wasn't speeding. When asked for his insurance papers, Patrick pulled a gun out of the glove box and shot both of the officers at point-blank range, killing them both. With the make and model of the truck given them by witnesses, the Highway Patrol set up roadblocks before Patrick could get away.

Patrick was tried and convicted of first-degree murder with special circumstances and sentenced to execution. A month later, he was killed with a shank by two of the other prisoners after threatening one of the inmates.

Shawna Amoretti was a woman in her mid-30s. She was happily married with two children, a boy and a girl, both in their teens. One evening, walking up the icy sidewalk in front of their Pittsburgh home, she fell and hit her head on the corner of their front step. She died in the ambulance on the way to the hospital. Paramedics were able to revive her and get her into the hospital.

They called a code blue almost immediately after she was taken into the emergency room. She stopped breathing. Emergency room doctors had to use electric paddles in order to restart her heart. She went into a coma for ten days.

After getting her home, Bruce, her husband began noticing a change in his wife. She had always been mild and seldom got mad. She started yelling at the kids and getting to the point where she was hitting them for little or no reason. Bruce consulted her doctors. They felt she may have injured the frontal lobe of her brain. As physicians could find no apparent damage, they recommended she see a psychiatrist and scheduled an appointment for the following week. As it turned out, that was much too late.

A couple of days later the police were summoned to their home by a neighbor. He said he heard arguing and gunshots coming from the neighbor's home and then the family car driving off. Police found the bodies of Bruce and the two kids on the living room sofa. All three had been shot at point-blank range. Detectives searched the rest of the house fearing to find Shawna's body. It was nowhere to be found.

Shauna was put at the top of their suspect list and an all-points bulletin was issued throughout the city. A convenience store was the scene of her next murder. She was caught on video shooting the sales clerk for no apparent reason. She then turned the gun on a man coming in the front door. She calmly went outside, put gas in her car and left.

Police assumed she got on the highway and left the state. Two days later three bodies were found at a campground near a large park. Ballistics showed the bullets killing the three came from the same gun that had killed Shauna's family and the store clerk. Realizing they had a serial killer on their hands, they stepped up police activity throughout the city.

Shauna's picture as well as the description and license number of the car she was driving, was featured on the front page of the newspaper the day after the campground killings. Police were called to a parking lot where her vehicle was spotted. As police arrived, Shawna's killing spree was in full swing. Four people lay mortally wounded outside their vehicles. Police shot and killed Shauna as she had her gun leveled on another victim.

This was a strange case for the police, as they could find absolutely no motive for the killings. Newspapers and the media had a field day, but things quieted down after a couple of days. In most cases of this type, the perpetrator has had a troubled life. In Shawna's case nothing could've been further from the truth. The family went to church every week and Shawna volunteered at a shelter. There was little doubt the problem was caused by her accident.

Murder, without cause, is probably the most mysterious of all crimes. Cases have been on the rise for several years. If criminals are not aware of security cameras, in many cases, they will kill their victims. With the death penalty being on the wane in most states, this is beginning to look more attractive to the criminal element.During the course of a year many prisoners are released to make room for the ever growing number of people committing murder. The police feel public involvement is crucial in bringing down these numbers. Everybody wants their family to feel safe, especially in their homes. For years police have been fighting an uphill battle to make that happen. Murder without motive is becoming more widespread all the time. The public needs to be more vigilant to illegal activities around them.

Chapter 26

A strange malady, that is not inherited, but sometimes becomes a reality when a person faces great danger is called "Stockholm syndrome". It was formerly called "normalmstorgsyndrome", named after normalmstorg bank in Stockholm Sweden.

Elin and Viktor Eke-Lund worked together in the normalmstorg bank in Stockholm Sweden. Elin was expecting their second child. In August of 1973 masked men came into the bank one morning, taking fifteen bank employees hostage, letting the customers out. These fifteen people, including Elin and Viktor, were held in the bank's vault for five days while the captors negotiated with police.

During that time, the hostages allied with their captors. This was probably caused by the stress each felt. They sensed their captors would probably kill them, which they threatened to do, if their demands were not met. Fearing physical harm or death, the anxiety these people felt caused them to identify with their captors. Even after the situation was over, several of the bank people sided with the captors. This was hard for police to understand.

This condition was coined "Stockholm syndrome" in the United States. Probably the most famous of these was the case of Patty Hearst, the granddaughter of William Randolph Hearst, a billionaire newspaperman. She was kidnapped from her Berkeley, California apartment and held for ransom by a man and wife team calling themselves the "Symbionese Liberation Army". This was started by a college professor at Berkeley California.

During her captivity, she allied with her captors. She was caught on videotape with a submachine gun, several times. After a period of nineteen months the FBI finally caught up with them. The house they were in was the second choice for the FBI. Jim Harrison, an agent for the FBI was on a stakeout at another location. This location was second choice for police. Jim and his partner soon determined this was where the criminals held out. SWAT teams were called out and subdued the three. Patty was tried and convicted of armed robbery and sentenced to life in prison. She was pardoned by President Bill Clinton, probably because of the uproar of several people feeling she wasn't to blame.

*****

A less known case of this involved Alvin Fisher. Al was a graduate student at the University of Arizona, Tucson. At twenty-two years old, he was popular on the campus. He studied music with Henry Johnson, a professor there, and former conductor of the Tucson Symphony orchestra.

Walking out of the class and down a walkway, Alvin was taken hostage by two men wearing hoods. The police figured the men had to be aware of class schedules in order to pull this off. Alvin's grandparents owned a chain of stores in and around Tucson. The police felt, this kidnapping was for ransom. They were correct. The kidnappers demanded a ransom of five hundred thousand dollars, threatening death to Alvin if the payment wasn't made.

Alvin was threatened and beaten into submission during the four days it took his grandparents to put together the cash needed. After two days, Alvin began to relate with his kidnappers. After the ransom was paid, Alvin was released, but refused to give testimony about his captors. His grandparents and police were not happy with his attitude. He claimed he knew nothing, and had forgotten most of it.

*****

Sue Byers and two of her friends were inside the market of a gas station outside of Albuquerque, New Mexico when two armed men, with masks, came in and shot the proprietor. While they were getting money from the cash register, an off-duty police officer happened to show up. As the two men started to exit the store, he drew his gun ordering them to put their hands up. Instead they closed the door, aiming their guns at the hostage's. Having heard the gunshot, the officer knew they meant business.

He called in and apprised his captain of the situation, and was ordered to stand down until more police units could arrive. The gunmen allowed EMTs to remove the proprietor from the store. The standoff which ensued lasted twenty-eight hours. During the time, they threatened to kill the women. Throughout their capture, a couple of the women began talking to these men. They even fixed sandwiches for them during the ordeal.

Ms. Byers was able to talk the men down explaining there was no way they were going to get out. She, and the other two women, told police the man who had been shot, raised a rifle to one of the robbers. They had not counted on the proprietor surviving his wounds. Their testimony, later proved false, and cost the women six months in jail for perjury.

*****

Frank Hall, a computer specialist for a large clothing manufacturer, was kidnapped in the parking lot of the business. He was taken to a dark room with a computer and ordered to give up proprietary information concerning the company he worked for. When he refused, he was beaten and tortured before he gave up the information the men were after.

As days rolled by, the victim became a participant in the crime. He started giving up information his captors hadn't asked for. Because of the valuable information he was able to give the criminal element; he asked for and was granted "a piece of the action".

Within two weeks' time he was catering to their every need. This included making plans for their getaway. As Frank had a family, he asked that the men release him, as information was given to them willingly. They granted this, and Frank never divulged to police what had happened, or where he was held, claiming he was blindfolded.

*****

Terry Blackmore worked at a small check-cashing firm. As she was gathering the day's receipts one evening, two men broke into the back of the store. Hearing the back door open, she immediately hit the button under the counter, calling the police. They were there before the two men could get away.

The two men grabbed Terry, threatening to kill her if the police didn't leave. They were not about to do that. The girl was taken into a back room and tied up. One of the men stayed with her near the back door while the other guarded the front. A seventeen hour standoff with SWAT officers did not produce results. The men were demanding transportation away from the site. The police did not comply with this.

Although Terry was terrified of being killed, she also began to relate to the men. By the time the ordeal was over, she had promised to help them with their legal fees as well as her testimony. The men realizing this was their only option gave into her. True to her word she kept her promise. To make matters worse, she had fallen in love with one of the men. The two were married, when he was released on good behavior, six months later.

*****

During a bank holdup in Midtown, Manhattan, bank employees and customers were taken to the vault and tied up, eight in all. A man trying to get in to the bank realized the door was locked, and called 911. The police showed up within minutes. Both back and front doors were closed off. SWAT officers showed up soon afterward.

A man, brandishing an AK-47, brought the bank manager out of the vault and to the front door. He threatened to kill the man, unless their demands were met. He wanted a getaway car, and clear passage to the airport. The telephone rang inside the bank and one of the gunmen answered it. He told the negotiator that he would kill a hostage every hour until his demands were met.

Because of the automatic weapons held by their captors, the captives began talking to the man inside the vault with them. At first they were told to be quiet, however with the first hour time limit coming up, the gunman began getting nervous. One of the hostages, taking a big chance, told the gunman, whether he pulled the trigger or not, taking the life of the bank manager, would be a probable death sentence for all three. Especially if any lives of the other hostages were taken as well.

One of the hostages started a conversation with the man, empathizing with his position. Some of the others in the vault, after a while, realized their fellow prisoner wasn't kidding. They began to wonder if he wasn't possibly in on it. He suggested the gunman close the door to the vault, so he wouldn't be so likely to be caught up in a murder conviction. Hearing the shot inside the bank, the gunman did just that.

Finding their cell phones wouldn't work in the vault, the assistant manager realized there was a landline in the vault. He immediately notified police the remaining hostages were all safe inside the locked vault, so they could take any action they deemed necessary. In just minutes they heard gunfire. They could hear pounding outside the vault door as one, or both of the gunmen tried to get in.

Both men were found mortally wounded by the hostages, when the door was opened. Hostages told police the gunman in the vault had saved their lives. They did not mention it wasn't his idea. The hostages were so traumatized by the experience; they felt nothing but high regard for their captor.

One of the outside gunmen was dead at the scene, the other rushed to the hospital where he died of his wounds hours later. The gunman in the vault was tried and convicted of second-degree manslaughter. Due to his actions, he was given ten years in prison, and released five years later on parole.

Long before the term "Stockholm syndrome" was coined, there were many cases of this. Before the Federal Reserve, (this was started by the banks). Many people lost their life savings when banks were held up, or made poor loans. Many times the people of the time would side with the bank robbers, not giving the bank or Marshall's information that could've led to the recovery of the stolen loot, providing it wasn't theirs.

Runs on the banks, when unsubstantiated rumors were being spread, caused banks to run out of money and without anything to back it up, closed their doors. When other banks were robbed, and hostages taken, many of these hostages would help the bandits escape.

Whether this help was given because the people were in fear for their lives, or just because of a general distrust of the banks at the time, we may never know. There is, however several instances when armed bandits were helped by hostages being held. The number of these cases may never be known.

Chapter 27

A problem with some people is the act to doing harm to themselves. This can be acts of financial sabotage or against one's physical being. When physical, these people are called cutters.

Margaret Mason was a young girl of fifteen. Since age 12 she had been cutting herself with her father's razor blades. Her parents were unaware of this as she always did the deed in places that couldn't be seen. Exactly what caused this compulsion is not known. Because of the way she was raised, she had low self-esteem. Whether or not this caused her condition is hard to say. It's a good bet it probably did.

In the beginning these cuts were shallow and barely drew blood. As time went on they began getting deeper, to the point where she had to put a bandage on them. This was becoming a daily ritual. She never felt she was beautiful enough to have any kind of relationship with a boy and consequently seldom dated.

When she got to the point of cutting her arms she had to wear long sleeve shirts and blouses. When her parents began to notice the bandages she had on her arms, they questioned her about this. She was able to claim they were accidental, cutting herself with a knife while preparing food. They accepted this explanation for a short time however; they soon began to realize she was having these "accidents" much too frequently. They realized she needed professional help and took her to a psychiatrist. He was able to negate her negative feelings of self-worth. She was soon cured of the compulsion.

*****

Greg Sorensen was a man in his early 20s. He began the practice of cutting himself at age 18 when a couple young girls he'd asked to the high school prom refused his invitation. This gave him a negative feeling of self-worth. How this type of rejection can affect a young man in this way is hard to say. It's not as uncommon as many people think, although this practice is much more common in young women.

Greg continued this practice using a sharp utility knife rather than razor blades, which are the most commonly used for cutters. He began to let up on this compulsion during a two-year stint in the Navy. He had pretty well stopped the practice by the time he was released. He met a young woman at a USO dance and the two fell in love.

Greg is now happily married with a child and works with young people who have problems with self-esteem and harming themselves. He understands how they feel giving him the confidence to do what is necessary to help them.

Linda Gucci, of Italian descent, began the practice of self-mutilation with a razor blade when her parents immigrated to the United States. She was twelve years old at the time. Here again, she had low self-esteem. She was popular in middle school and had many friends. She kept her obsession to herself. Excuses in her gym class were accepted by her fellow classmates, but not so much by her instructor.

She was sent to counseling by the school psychologist. This helped her immensely. The psychologist referred her parents to a psychiatrist who explained to her that with her many friends she was a good person. She was lucky in that she was able to break her compulsion after a few months of treatment.

*****

Derek Smith had this compulsion of harming himself as well. However his compulsion was different than those who harmed themselves physically. By an early age he started to become wealthy.

This presented a problem as Derek felt it came too easy and he didn't deserve it. He began to sabotage financial dealings that he made, knowingly getting into bad investments. Within a couple of years, he was practically living on the streets. He had always been too busy to consider marriage or a family. Although he was handsome, he never went out of his way to attract a mate. He bounced around in this financial condition, taking on small maintenance jobs in the low income apartment building where he lived.

Doing repair work under a sink in one of the units, he noticed an attractive set of legs walking into the kitchen. He had seen this girl from time to time and was physically attracted to her. He felt embarrassed even talking to her in his financial state. That problem was taken care of when she sat on a kitchen chair and began a conversation with him.

He began to realize it didn't take wealth to make a man. At that point he began a financial comeback. His portfolio, as before, grew exponentially as time went on. Within six months he felt he could afford a family and asked Susan out on a serious date. Up to that point it had just been a cup of coffee in her apartment. He is now happily married with two sons. Unlike a lot of men, he's never let his success in business get in the way of his family. He's passed that on to his sons.

*****

Sondra Manson was a woman in her 30s. She had a lucrative business as a dress designer. She had three girls working for her in a dress shop as well. She thought the money would make her happy. It didn't, and she knew she had to do something about that. The obsession with money is a common one. Not quite so common, is feeling the need to get rid of it. She began to realize her obsession for wealth had cost her happiness in life. They say money can't buy happiness, but it can make misery more enjoyable. However when that need becomes a compulsion, it can ruin one's life.

Sondra began giving her wealth to charities helping the underprivileged. This gave her a sense of self-worth which she had never felt before in her life. As strange as it seems, she began to feel happiness. She sold her elaborate apartment and moved into a condominium which she had purchased. She was beginning to feel satisfied with herself.

Within a couple of years, she met and married a man who she fell in love with. She now has what she craved, a family. Truth be told, she often misses her old way of life, and certainly the financial attributes, but she is now happier than before, and for her that's what counts.

*****

Peter Michaels had a low opinion of himself from the time he was getting into puberty. He felt he had no right to be happy. This was due to the way he was raised. He tried to help his father in every respect; however, nothing he did was good enough to please his dad.

He began putting himself into dangerous situations. His classmates thought he was just being brave, but he was constantly trying to hurt himself. Walking against traffic signals going to and from school, purposely walking in front of trains and walking on the edge of bridges were just a few examples.

Peter relished getting into the military and going overseas on active duty. He began putting himself in harm's way at every opportunity. He was always the first to volunteer to go out and look for insurgents. This insanity ended when he was shot and almost died. He finally got his wish of wanting to hurt himself. He was sent back to the United States, to Johns Hopkins Hospital. His leg was amputated above the knee. He was fitted with an artificial leg. He lost his taste for getting into harm's way.

After six months he is now getting rigorous physical therapy to allow him to get back on his feet again. The Purple Heart he was awarded gives him little comfort.

Chapter 28

William Chatsworth is referred to as a narcissistic sociopath. He believes the world revolves around him. Although having illegal activities on the side, he also ran a lucrative car business. As a deacon in the local church, he was highly respected by its members. He always felt he was far above everybody else in the community. This didn't always play well with friends and family.

He was not above acts of first-degree murder in his illegal activities. Some of these involved drug trade as well as gunrunning. He was involved in the murders of four of his competitors. He justified this, feeling he was doing the world a favor getting rid of them.

The police and community never considered him a suspect in any of these murders. Besides the four he committed himself, twelve others were committed at his command. The bodies were taken out and dumped in landfills around the city. He always saw to it, others did the dirty work. His reputation came to an end when he stabbed a man in a bar fight. Witnesses claimed it was William's fault. The man later died and William was charged with second-degree murder.

This opened the floodgates as some of his illegal activities began coming to light. The car dealership was sold to pay his legal fees, which were staggering. As the court trial continued, some of his partners in crime began coming forward, anonymously, accusing him in the murders and giving locations of the victims.

He was acquitted of the stabbing, but sentenced to death by lethal injection for the killings. Unfortunately for Peter, no deals could be made, and he died in the state prison at midnight, six years later.

*****

Marty Hansen was a good looking young lady in her 20s. She knew she was attractive to men. She felt she could get away with anything and did for a few years. She would lure prominent men to her apartment; blackmail them, threatening them with exposure and humiliation. Some of her customers were high ranking members of state and federal government. They all had reputations to protect.

She had a few judges on the string. Some of the superior court judges as well. She certainly had a good thing going. Within a few years she was living in an exclusive condominium and had a sizable bank account. There were also stocks and bonds in her portfolio. Some of her clients were prominent stockbrokers, and due to insider trading, she was able to increase her wealth exponentially.

When one of her clients, a prominent judge, died of a heart attack in her arms, her schemes came to an end. Going back into transcripts, investigators found evidence of her illegal deeds. She knew she would be doing a lot of prison time through her activities with the Justice Department.

To bring down her jail time, she gave the authorities her little black book. The names in that book caused misery to many of her clients in high places. Some of them were sent to prison for their illegal activities, especially in the stocks and bonds trade. The money Marty had made in these activities was removed from her bank account. This also included stocks and bonds held in her name.

There's little doubt she was a sociopath. Being narcissistic she always put herself above everybody else. This certainly included her clients whom she looked down on as being weak. The fact that many of these men were powerful, gave her that much more a feeling of self-worth. Because of her testimony she was given probation after two years in prison.

*****

Jodi Jenkins was a homicidal psychopath. The man whom she had met taking her dog in to be neutered, was a veterinarian in Carson City,

Nevada. It seemed to her, over the next two days, her dog was getting a lot more attention than the other animals. She took this as a sign, that the doctor was infatuated with her. She spent the next three days learning everything she could about him over the Internet. He was single and had just moved into town from the Midwest. She started making excuses to go back to his office needing advice on the care of her pet.

Bill Franklin was infatuated by her and the attention she was showing him. He started dating her, but as a friend. There were other women out there who he dated from time to time. She turned a blind eye to his other girlfriends, thinking of them as bitches and whores.

Jodi thought he may take them out from time to time in order to make her jealous. She managed to get him into the bedroom, and at that point assumed he was hers. Unfortunately, for him, he didn't see it that way. He told her on more than one occasion he wanted her as a friend, even though most of their dates wound up back in his bedroom.

She began getting stars in her eyes and brought up the subject of marriage. Being a young bachelor, he wanted to sow some wild oats. However, he wasn't ready for that serious a relationship with anybody. He made the mistake of telling her so. He decided it would be best if they parted company for a few weeks to think about things. She agreed to that, but began stalking him.

Within two weeks she was back in his bedroom. They both enjoyed each other, however she wasn't quite what he was looking for, she being a little rough around the edges.

It took her a while to understand where he was coming from, and she began to realize their relationship was at a dead end. She did not like being pushed aside for somebody else. In one of her numerous rendezvous', showing up at his home unexpectedly one night, she caught him having a glass of wine with another woman, on his sofa. This did not play well with her.

A couple of nights later she invited herself into his home once more. As he was pouring a couple glasses of wine, she came behind him with a knife and started stabbing him multiple times in the back and neck. When he refused to die, she moved the knife to his throat, practically decapitating him. Afterwards she put a bullet through his heart for good measure. She then leisurely went back to her car.

As is the case with most psychopaths, she felt justified in what she had done. Police didn't see it that way, and soon caught up to her. She was sentenced to life without parole, in a mental institution.

Psychopaths who murder their partners out of love are more often women than men. Most men that do this act use a gun rather than a knife.

Claude Mariano came from the old country of Italy, a few years before. He, like most men from other countries, felt a woman should do what she's told. Not exactly a concept that is embraced by women in the United States. He picked Marcy up in a Catholic Church. He felt a woman with a religious upbringing would satisfy his needs.

She agreed to see him for coffee that afternoon after church. She felt he, being a gentle man, would be fun to go out with. She didn't realize that he, like most men, was only showing her his good side.

His invitations soon included dinner in some of the better nightspots. He was financially secure, having sold his grocery business in Italy before immigrating. She liked him, but dated other men from time to time. After a while, he told her he didn't want her seeing anybody else. She told him it was too early to make that decision, just yet. He left that night, and went home in a rage of anger and disappointment.

Two nights later Claude confronted her on the front porch of her home. She told him she had not changed her mind and wanted to date other men on occasion. She was about to find out that was a bad mistake on her part. He pushed her through the front door and onto the living room floor. She looked up in terror as he drew out a gun and put two bullets into her chest. She died instantly.

Claude was charged with first-degree murder and sentenced to death. Having a battery of lawyers, he was able to get that sentence commuted to life in prison, with no possibility of parole. He was killed in a prison brawl two months later.

Although the majority of murders in this way are during fits of anger and rage, some are accidental, and some planned out, being careful of details to avoid prosecution,

One such case was Robert Palermo. He went to great lengths to be sure he would never be convicted of the murder he planned for his ex-girlfriend. Sheila had moved on to greener pastures, telling him in essence, to get lost. He told her he was leaving for California. On the night they broke up he put something into her drink before leaving the restaurant. She was dead fifteen hours later. This was a form of arsenic poisoning which left the system almost immediately upon the death of the individual.

Although Sheila was healthy, **the coroner ruled it death by heart attack.** Because Robert could prove he was in Utah at the time, nobody looked at him as a suspect. Neighbors told police detectives as far as they knew, the couple was happy, and planning marriage. Nothing could have been further from the truth, but they didn't know it.

At the insistence of Sheila's sister, Anna Mae, detectives decided to look into her sister's death a little more closely. Doctors and morgue officials did just that. Using special tools and forensic techniques they were able to find trace amounts of the poison in her system. The waitress at the bar where they had their final drink, told detectives Sheila went into the restroom and came back out and finished her drink shortly before leaving. She also said the man Sheila was with left minutes before.

Pictures shown the waitress positively identified Robert Palermo as being in the restaurant with her. He was picked up in California and extradited back. Along with other evidence, Palermo was convicted of first-degree murder and sentenced to life without the possibility of parole. The case is still under review.

*****

Another strange case of a homicidal sociopath, took place in a large Catholic Church in the middle of Boston. A young woman, Brenda Lee Ward was found guilty of first-degree homicide. She had gone to confession one morning and given what she felt was good advice on a matter of love between her and her boyfriend. The priest, father Antonio had advised her to leave the man, as he was much older than her and frequently abused her.

Her reasons never understood, Brenda Lee took this as an invitation by the priest to become her new boyfriend. Being a man of the cloth he had no intention of doing this, but on the other hand didn't want to hurt her feelings. He began sitting with her at coffee clutches after church services on Sunday mornings and Wednesday nights. She took this as an act of love on his part and felt that way towards him as well. He was not about to forsake his vows for anybody. He liked the girl and felt he was helping her get through a bad time. Unfortunately, she didn't quite see it that way. She had fallen in love with the man.

He had gently tried to explain to her that as a priest he was devoted to God and could not take a wife. Trying to let her down gently, he explained it again. At another table that Sunday morning, he was talking to one of the other female parishioners as Brenda Lee looked on in shame and disgust. Later in the day, she returned to the church where father Antonio was setting up for the evening services. She asked that he hear her confession. He agreed and followed her into a confessional booth.

That evening a couple of the church members saw blood coming out of the base of the confessional. When the door was opened, father Antonio's body fell to the floor in a pool of his blood. It didn't take long for detectives to piece together what had happened. After psychiatric examination, it was found because of her mental state at the time; Brenda Lee would spend the rest of her life in a hospital for the criminally insane.

The feeling of rejection is one of the most upsetting feelings a person can have. In a lot of cases these feelings start as a child. Most go away as time goes on. This is true in later life as well. Some people don't handle rejection very well. It's not often this will result in someone being killed, but it does happen.

Love is probably the greatest experience humans have for each other. It's heartbreaking when it goes in only one direction, tragic when it becomes an obsession.

Lisa Collins had several one night stands with guys who had picked her up in bars. All of the guys were nice to her and she took that as a sign of falling in love with her. One man, Gary Martin, was an exception. He was a junior partner for a firm she worked for as a systems analyst.

She was attracted to his physique and the fact that he was a kind person. One evening she was working late when he came out of his office. They had enjoyed Small-talk in the past from time to time. He came over to where she was working to say good night to her. As she was just cleaning things up getting ready to go home, he asked her if she might enjoy dinner with him that night. She happily accepted this kind offer and they left the building for a buffet down the street.

He was polite to her and didn't come on strong as most men did with her. This attracted her as she wasn't used to being treated in this manner. During their meal she mentioned having problems with her neck and shoulders and that it had been a few days since she'd been able to move her head comfortably. She thought it was probably from constantly working on the computer. He told her he knew how to fix that.

They took a taxicab to her apartment, and stopped by the drugstore to pick up a few things on the way. Going into her apartment, he suggested she go in and get into a hot bath and then come into her bedroom where he'd be waiting for her. She agreed and thought this was just going to be another one of those dates. She couldn't have been more wrong.

When she came into the bedroom with a towel wrapped around her body, he motioned her over to the bed. She was surprised the only thing he had removed was his jacket. The night stands on each side of the bed held a candle which he had picked up at the drugstore along with a bottle of massage oil. He had warmed it in hot water from the kitchen sink. He got a bed sheet from her closet which he lay on the bed and had her lie down on her stomach. He asked her to move the towel down to her waist, which she did. She was beginning to get an inkling of his idea of foreplay.

Putting the lotion on his strong hands, he began massaging the oil onto her neck and upper arms. With both thumbs he pushed hard on the upper part of her spine in an upward motion, which he repeated several times. This was a little painful, but she could feel the results. He had her begin to move her head back and forth, which she did. At that point she realized the tension in her neck and shoulders was gone and she could freely move her head. He continued with the oil going downward massaging her upper back, slowly making his way down to her waist.

He continued his ministrations down the back of her thighs and calves and ankles before turning her over on her back. She was sure he would have her remove the towel but she was wrong. He worked his way up her calves and thighs and stopped at the appropriate place. He then went to her neck. She, like most women usually got uncomfortable at this point but she trusted him fully. He massaged her neck and worked his way down rubbing the globes of her breasts until she purred like a Kitten.

He continued down to her navel slowly massaging every nook and cranny of her body. At that point he told her to roll over on her stomach and get comfortable, which she did. He removed the towel and massaged her backside. She was more than ready for him. He gave her a friendly pat on her rump.

At that point he got her a glass of red wine which he had picked up from the side-table. She sat on the edge of the bed with him. After they were through with the wine, he gave her a kiss on her forehead, put on his jacket, said good night and left. This was on the complete opposite end of the spectrum she was expecting. She put on her nightgown and went to bed wondering what she had done wrong. At this point she knew she was in love with him.

The next day at the office, Gary stopped at her desk and said hello to her and asked how her neck was doing. She told him she was feeling great and thanked him for what he had done the night before. He then proceeded to his office and closed the door. She had stars in her eyes, but couldn't quite figure him out. She thought he must just be shy.

Within a couple days of Smalltalk and coffee, she was able to get him back up to her apartment. Although he was a religious man, which she was not, she managed to get him in the bedroom for more than just the massage. He had specifically told her they were friends and that was it. This time she lit the candles and poured them both a glass of wine. They made love in much the way he had given her the massage a few nights back. He knew all the right buttons to push, and pushed them. They made love for the next couple of hours and fell asleep.

Being Saturday morning they had a repeat performance of the night before. She got up and fixed breakfast for him while he was taking a shower. They enjoyed each other's company most of the morning. He left about noon telling her he'd see her at the office Monday morning. That wasn't quite what she had in mind, but she accepted it.

After a couple of weeks, Gary began to realize something was wrong. He liked her a lot, but love wasn't in the cards for him. She had forgotten all about their little agreement on that first night. She couldn't get Gary out of her mind and became obsessed with him. He began to make excuses for not going home with her and their trysts became less frequent. She became infuriated when she saw him talking to any female in the office pool. He finally decided he'd had enough, and broke it off with her.

She became incensed over Gary's behavior towards her. After a couple of weeks she followed him to his home. She met him at the front porch asking that they may talk. He invited her in, removing his jacket and throwing it on the couch. His home was very well kept.

She asked him if they could get back together again. He steadfastly refused telling her he appreciated her friendship; however would not allow a relationship with her to go any further than that.

As he walked to the kitchen, she pulled a gun from her bag and shot him twice in the back. As he lay dying, she explained to him that if she couldn't have him, neither could anyone else. The neighbors had called the police when they heard the gunshots. Officers found her sitting in a pool of blood next to him, on the floor, in tears. She was tried and convicted of first-degree murder and sent to prison for the rest of her natural life.

Alex Manes never had much luck with the ladies. He was highly intelligent and taught calculus at the state college in nearby Reno Nevada. One of his older students caught his eye. As she was having a bit of trouble in class he offered to help her after class. She accepted and they got to know each other and became friends. He asked her out to dinner one evening, and she said yes. He thought he'd finally found the girl of his dreams. Over the course of the next two months, until the end of the semester, they continued to see each other, however it never became physical.

Wanda was a pretty girl and at age 28 was taking refresher courses at the college to better herself as an employee at her brother-in-law's firm. She had gotten out of a bad marriage a couple years before and didn't want a repeat performance of that with anybody. She liked Alex very much, but did not feel romantic love for him. He had tried on several occasions to get together with her in the biblical way. He was not adept at this sort of thing.

He began noticing her attention shifting from him to a couple of other men on campus. His jealousy ignited. One night he followed her to her home and shot her in the back with a rifle as she walked through the front door. He then sped away.

As police questioned neighbors, they found no witness to the crime. They all told police Wanda was friendly to them and never had a bad word to say about anybody, that they knew of. They were aware of the fact that she had been dating one of the men at the college, but beyond that could tell them nothing.

Two of the men she had been seeing were brought into police headquarters for questioning. One had a solid alibi for the night of the murder, the other did not. He said he was back in his room studying. He did however mention that Yolanda had been dating one of her college professors.

Questioning several students around the campus, detectives were led to Alex Manes office. He denied having anything to do with it, however police were not convinced. They got a search warrant for his home where they found the rifle that had been used to commit Yolanda's murder. He was tried and convicted of first-degree murder and sentenced to death by lethal injection. That sentence was carried out ten years later, after exhausting all pleas for leniency.

There have been many cases like this. People don't usually go to the extreme of murder; however some make things very uncomfortable for those who have jilted them. One such case was in Tucson, Arizona.

Fred and Martha met at a runners club. Both were in fine physical condition. On occasion, Fred would invite her into a small bakery nearby, for coffee and a donut. They would often kid about having to run that extra mile to justify the donut. Fred liked to kid around with her. Unfortunately she sometimes took these jests as being serious.

After a time the relationship became physical. Her apartment was nearby, so their afternoon playtime had easy access for them. Martha wanted to make this a permanent relationship; Fred did not. Reluctantly she agreed to keep their relationship as it was. This went on for a couple weeks until an accidental meeting at a supermarket.

Fred was there with another woman, who turned out to be his wife. Two young children accompanied them as well. Fred was embarrassed, Martha incensed. He was able to get her off by herself and apologized for his deception. This was far from enough to satisfy Martha. She confronted Fred's wife, as he stood there red-faced.

That evening, after getting home, Fred apologized many times for what he had done. His wife would forgive him, however he'd be sleeping on the couch for a while. She began insisting on other things as well. Fred was not about to leave her and the kids, so he complied with these. Several appliances were bought, rooms painted, as well as other odds and ends. Fred had learned his lesson.

Martha was able to go on with her life as well, this time being sure there was no wife or kids involved. She went on to meet and marry one of the other men in the club. Fred was never seen there again.

One way love is probably the most tragic of all types for both. One partner is trying to figure out what they did wrong, while the other doesn't want to hurt his or her friend, but cannot see a lifetime living with them. In most cases both go on to find more suitable partners. It's unfortunate the misery that can ensue in the meantime. Men and women are intended to be together to propagate the human race. Marriage is the idea of the church. It's a good thing, especially when children are involved. Divorce rates in this country are high, especially in good economic times when a wife isn't quite so dependent on her husband. This becomes a tragedy when children are involved, as they often become property for their parents to fight over. In good marriages, the entire family has good reason to be happy.

Part two.   Chapter-30-- Phobias

....

Human phobias are varied and many. In many respects they mirror compulsive behaviors. They are irrational, excessive and persistent fears and fall in all sorts of categories.

Fear of insanity

Agate-phobia is a fear of becoming insane or contracting Alzheimer's disease. This fear is most prevalent when other family members are stricken by this.

In one such case, Marlene Davies had this phobia. Because of this, she remained unmarried for life. Psychologists as well as psychiatrists had treated her over the years. She was still convinced that she had this genetic predisposition. This was strange as she had a job teaching history in the local high school.

Her social life was confined mostly to parties and get-togethers with other family members. Although she was encouraged to marry and have a family, she rejected the suggestions to do so. She continued her teaching career, but remained single for life. She did not want to take a chance on passing this to future generations.

Fred Jackson was a man in his early 30s. His social life had been limited to meeting friends and co-workers at local bars. His father, whom he often visited, was in an institution for the criminally insane.

He began spending too much time after work in the bars. He began drinking more than normal and talking about things he had done earlier in his life. His co-workers began getting uncomfortable around him and quit coming in for their nightly drinking sessions. In his earlier life he had beat his wife to death. This caused him to go on a compulsive rampage, raping and killing three more women.

After having himself castrated so as not to pass on his genes he was caught and sentenced to life in prison. He was soon on a downward spiral. At age 40, he wrote a note to his family apologizing for his actions, and explained he had an intense fear of going insane. Prison personnel found him hanging from the end of a rope in his jail cell.

As an unhappy footnote, during the autopsy on his brain, doctors found him to be genetically sound. In his case, death was definitely from fear.

••

Fear of nakedness

Dishabiliophobia or the fear of undressing or being naked in front of anybody is normal, until one is married. There are numerous cases of people, mostly women, with this disorder.

Probably the most notorious of these cases was several years ago. Mrs. McCarty ran a daycare center in Los Angeles. Some of the children in the school began accusing her of coming into the school room stark naked. Her husband refuted that, saying in their thirty years of marriage, he was yet to see her with no clothes on. When the case was looked into by her attorneys, it was found that one of the children had kiddingly told his parents that his teacher was performing acts of lewd conduct in the classroom. Although acquitted of all charges, the McCarthy's closed down the school.

Rick Hart had this obsession as well. In his junior high school years, his gym class was a constant embarrassment. It was his first experience being naked in front of anybody, with the exception of his parents. During the first year his parents noticed he was becoming more despondent with each passing day. As much as they tried to talk to him, it was apparent their conversations were not getting through.

They sent him to the school psychologist. She in turn wrote to the coach in the gym class stating that his condition could not improve as long as he was subjected to other students seeing him naked. For this reason he was given a deferment from gym class. This went on through his high school years as well.

Although Rick Hart became happily married with children, his wife never saw him nude. He always undressed himself under the covers and pulled on his pajama bottoms, or shorts, before getting out of bed. This obsession stayed with him for several years, before he was finally able to break it, with the help of a psychiatrist.

Julie Rogers, even as a child, felt uncomfortable being naked around her parents. At age 5 they noticed it, especially when giving her a bath. She asked that she bathe or shower alone, which her parents granted. Her parents noticed she was becoming obsessed with this, in all stages of her life. In her junior high school years, her parents were asked to come in and speak to the Vice Principal. Julie's coach in physical education class told them Julie refused to undress in front of the class. The fact all the other kids were doing it, made no difference to her.

Julie saw a school guidance counselor about this. The counselor suggested she see a psychologist to ease the problem. It took several months of rigorous sessions, but Julie was helped. Once realizing this was an unhealthy compulsion, she made a concerted effort to curb it. By the age of eighteen, she was considered normal. She married and had two children of her own. She still feels uncomfortable undressing in front of her husband.

Donnie Savion became distraught in high school gym class from remarks made by other students. In a teasing manner, they remarked about the size of his organ. This came to the point where he developed a phobia about anybody seeing it. At age 25 he never forgot the remarks made and went to a student counselor demanding he be excused from class. From that day forward nobody had ever seen him naked. Never married, he stayed celibate for life.

It's common for people to become embarrassed when nude in front of anybody, especially the opposite sex. Some people even feel uncomfortable undressing in front of their doctors. This is not considered an obsession until it takes control of your life.

There are people on the other side of the fence. Some men and women alike, get a perverse thrill out of shocking people by parading around in front of them in the nude. This is more in line with a fetish and will be dealt with later.

Eisoptrophobia

Kristi Wells suffered from a similar phobia; Eisoptrophobia is a fear of mirrors, and seeing oneself in the mirror. People with horrible disfigurement's, usually from automobile, or other types, of accidents, are most prone to this condition.

Kristi wells was an intelligent young lady, but for no apparent reason suffered from this phobia. In getting ready for school, she had her mother do her face and hair. After she outgrew that, she began doing it for herself, using the mirror only when necessary. She always asked her mother if she looked okay, before going out.

Up to that point, her parents didn't have a clue that mirrors bothered her. She willingly went to a psychiatrist for this and after a time was considered cured. She still resisted looking at mirrors, but was able to face herself in them when necessary.

Billy Ferguson was cursed with this problem as well. He had a disfigurement of the face, caused at an earlier age from his brain swelling at two quick a pace. His doctors were able to control the swelling, however they discouraged plastic surgery.

During his school years he insisted on wearing a partial mask. His teachers and fellow students understood his reasons for this. Although it had been drilled into him for many years that looks meant little, he realized they did.

He never married, and unfortunately at age 30, succumbed to his illness. Vanity is more than capable of ruining one's life.

Marjorie Kaman had a serious automobile accident at age 19. This disfigured her face. Thinking her life was over; she tried to commit suicide on two occasions. Her weight got out of hand because of this, as well. She developed a fear of looking in mirrors. It got to the point where every time she looked in the mirror, she saw more things wrong with her face.

Marjorie got to the point where she thought everybody was watching her all the time in disgust. In reality nothing could have been further from the truth. As in most cases, people looking at her felt pity for her. It's human nature to not be happy with one's looks, unless of course you're on the other side of the fence and are narcissistic.

Unless friends or family say otherwise, most of us are in the middle of the road on this one. There are likely things that were not happy with, on the other hand don't really mind it enough to change.

*****

Gynophobia

Gynophobia is an intense fear of women. In most cases this phobia stems from an overbearing mother during childhood. A Gynophobic is afraid to get involved with, and in some severe cases get near a woman. This can be due to thinking one's sex organs or knowledge of sex will not be sufficient to satisfy them. The majority of these cases are men.

....

Gynophobia has little if anything to do with homosexuality. A lot of gay men get along very well with women and vice versa.

For year's twenty-eight-year-old Bill Jennings thought he may be gay, although he never felt attracted to another man. He did, on the other hand, have an intense fear of being close to women. This presented a real problem as many people working with him in the law firm, where he was employed as a file clerk, were women. He felt uncomfortable around them and they quickly learned to give him space.

This affected him physically as well as mentally as he would become progressively sick being too close to them. The law firm he worked for wanted to keep him, and consequently gave him an office of his own. There he kept all the necessary files on the cases they handled, as well as computer logs.

After this phobia became too much for him, he consulted a psychiatrist. Within a couple of years he could approach a woman with no ill effects. He still had no desire for physical contact with them.

In some cases female siblings, especially if there is more than one in the household, will make a boy feel inadequate in a lot of ways. Criticizing his every move regardless of whether or not he's doing them right, can definitely contribute to this condition.

Stephen Anderson was happily married with no children. The love he felt for his wife, over the first years of marriage, began to wane as they remained childless.

She began to question his manhood. His doctor informed him that his tests showed week sperm counts. His wife insisted on divorce, and he later found she had been having affairs outside of the marriage.

He became totally distrustful of all women after his divorce. Not even psychiatry could shake this feeling of fear when he was around them. This later resulted in his taking his own life by a gunshot to the head.

These are extreme examples of Gynophobia. In the majority of cases psychological tests and sessions, with a qualified psychiatrist, can curb, or cure the condition.

••

Demo-phobia

•••

Demo phobia sometimes referred to as Enoclo-phobia, is the term associated with an intense fear of being in crowds of people. This is not to be confused with claustrophobia, which will be mentioned later. Because of this condition, some people will become agoraphobic and consequently not able to leave their homes.

Sally Fielding became lost as a child in a major shopping center, during the Christmas holidays, Christmas is shoppers were out in droves. She was told to hang on to her mother's hand, which became impossible when her mother was trying on a new dress in one of the cubicles.

Sally was told to stay in the chair outside the room, but like most children got impatient and wanted to see Christmas toys. Her mother became frantic when the child was not sitting where she was told. Loudspeakers in the store, told her to go to a cashier's desk. She became panicked when she couldn't find one. Crowds of shoppers blocked her view and kept bumping into her in all directions.

This day subconsciously, more than any other, contributed to her condition. It wasn't until a legitimate hypnotist was found, that she could let go of those subconscious feelings and return to a healthy environment. She remained normal for the rest of her life.

Thomas Hayes had the condition as well. In spite of this, he became a top drawer scientist and moved to the Alaska wilderness. In the capacity of his knowledge of underwater science, he worked for the US geological survey there. As there were only five other employees, it was his ideal location.

He became uncomfortable when government officials would, on occasion, come to the installation. For the most part he remained calm and stayed in the job until retirement. At that point he became a hermit in the wilderness of Alaska until his death at age 84.

Judy Williams developed an intense fear of crowds after having her pocket picked leaving a packed stadium. She wasn't injured, however lost about fifteen hundred dollars in cash, as well as credit cards. She did recover from this to help of psychiatry, and no longer carries cash.

There are a lot of us that do not like being in crowds. Reasons for this can range anywhere from being lost in a store full of people, to being in a hurry to get to the car. This is normal for many people.

Claustrophobia

Claustrophobia and is a fear of being inside enclosed places, especially elevators. This can present a real problem for people working or living in high-rise buildings. It is a condition which can be lessened or in some cases, cured through psychological help.

Erin Michaels was a woman with that problem. Even bathrooms, that were not well lit, caused her anxiety. She had a spacious apartment on the ground floor of a Milwaukee, Wisconsin building. Her biggest problem was her reliance on the train taking her to and from work. She always took a window seat with a lot of light which helped.

When she met her husband to be, their first date was in the dark lounge of a restaurant. She began to perspire heavily and became nauseous before her date realized something was wrong. He immediately called for the check and asked that they be moved into the restaurant. That solved her problem. Although seeing psychologists, the problem would remain with her for years to come.

Richard Barnes had a problem even being in an elevator lobby. This did not manifest itself until he was in his 20s, going down in an elevator from his work on the thirtieth floor. The elevator cable became jammed and broke. This resulted in the elevator dropping until the automatic break stopped it two floors below. He soon found another job which did not require the use of an elevator. He has never been in one since. One can easily understand his reasons for this even though accidents of this nature rarely happen.

Claustrophobia, to a certain extent, can affect almost anybody. Even some of the astronauts have experienced difficulty at times with this. It is common for many of us not to enjoy closed-in spaces.

Jean Merrick had a severe case of claustrophobia. Riding or driving in a vehicle for more than a couple miles would cause her to break out in sweat. The sight of elevators could cause bouts of anxiety. When in the restroom in her home, she had to leave the door open. As she didn't have children, that wasn't a problem for her. Her husband understood her condition and helped her in every way possible.

A breakthrough came when he read an article that explained this condition and recommended psychiatric help for it. A hypnotist working in the office gave her posthypnotic suggestions. Through these and other sessions, he determined the cause of her problems. She had been left in the backseat of her car while her mother was shopping. She was two years old at the time. The windows were closed, and she almost died from the heat. These sessions solved her problem.

Buried alive

••

Even scarier than death is the thought of being buried alive or Tap phobia. This has probably occurred to all of us at one time or another. In this day of modern medicine, it's almost impossible for anything like this to happen. In the eighteenth century alone, over two hundred and fifty cases of Tap phobia were proven when bodies were exhumed for one reason or another.

In earlier days as a preventative measure to this, glass lids were often installed in caskets and left above ground for several days for observation. Bells attached to ropes going up the grave markers could be rung. In some instances, breathing tubes could be installed to ensure being able to breathe. These two answers left little hope for those buried, as somebody would have to be around when the incidents occurred. Graveyards are not usually that well populated.

There have been approximately a hundred and fifty incidents in history, however, where these measures saved somebody's life.

Some stories claimed this happened to Abraham Lincoln, pulling the rope on the Bell, when he was about twenty years of age. Whether that actually happened or not is hard to say.

I doubt that anybody has not thought about what could happen under the circumstances if they, themselves were in that coffin. In this day and age that can be ruled "almost" impossible.

In the year nineteen hundred, John Fox was laid to rest in his hometown of Vienna, Austria. He had been the victim of the flu epidemic. At the time the disease was running rampant worldwide. After he was diagnosed having the flu, he was hospitalized where he went into a coma.

As he was going into the ground, the priest presiding over the funeral heard tapping and other noises coming from inside the coffin. The coffin was quickly lifted and the lid opened. John had been saved from a horrifying death.

Unfortunately for many victims of frontier justice, this would not have been the case. Although they may have stopped breathing, bandits, horse thieves or cattle wrestlers were hanged out on the prairie anywhere near trees. They were often buried nearby in makeshift graves. It's hard to say how many of these men were not actually dead when they were buried.

Fear of Death

The fear of death or Necrophilia affects all of us, man and beast alike. It is said that nobody wants to die, but everyone wants to go to heaven. Death is a natural part of living and probably should not be feared. However, that's a lot easier to say, than to believe.

Most all religions on earth profess knowledge of knowing what happens when one dies. Facing facts, nobody really does. There have been stories of people dying, especially on operating tables, and then being brought back to life. After the experience a lot of these people claim to no longer fear death. It's very comforting to know this, but the fact is nobody is really dead until the brain dies.

A lot of us spend a lifetime searching for the meaning of life. In many, this becomes the driving force of our life. Is there a God out there? Most of us want to believe there is. A lot of people, especially in science and medicine, do not have that belief. How anybody can look at a simple tree, or x-rays showing inside the human body, and think that we were some sort of a cosmic accident, is beyond this author's imagination.

•••

Fear of growing old

The fear of growing old, Gerascophobia's, is probably instilled in all of us. One might say it sure beats the alternative.

In many, the fear isn't so much of getting old, as getting there alone. As medical science increases longevity, more and more people, especially women, are outgrowing their spouses. In many cases like these, friends can be a godsend.

Stephen Ferris, a man of ninety, lost his wife to cancer five years before. They had been married for seventy years. They had a good marriage, which included four children, eighteen grandchildren, five great grandchildren and two great-great grandchildren. Their visits to a retirement home he resided in became his biggest joy in life.

Around the holidays he would become despondent. He was often invited to one of his family's homes at Thanksgiving, Christmas and other holidays. Several relatives in the state asked that he come live with them. Knowing the fallacy in that, he declined their invitations. He was one of the lucky ones.

Geraldine Larch was not so lucky. She lived in a single bedroom apartment. All of her family had either died or moved away. After a year, telephone calls became scarce. They did send cards at her birthday and Christmas. She saved all of these in a dresser drawer. At age 80, her health began to decline.

They say it takes health, love and money to make one happy. She had lost all three. Living on Social Security from her husband's meager job, she was living in abject poverty. She was too proud to accept subsistence from the state, having been raised to feel that was a sin. Her strong belief in God kept her going since her husband's death. Now, realizing death was imminent; she threw herself into the Bible, for comfort.

She was found dead a few months later when failing to pay her monthly rent. Her building manager found her lying on the couch, the holy Bible clutched in her hands.

It's natural for human beings to fear the unknown. Some people suffering from a terminal illness, their body racked with pain, welcome the day it's over. At one point, we're all going to die. The trick is holding that off as long as possible.

Fear of dark places

••

Achluo-phobia or a fear of dark places is common among young children, imagining monsters hiding under their bed, or in the closet. The child will usually grow out of this as he or she gets older. This phobia can affect women that have been pulled into dark alleys as well. Men rarely have the problem, but, there are cases out there.

Billy Richter was a young boy five years of age. Up to that point he hadn't had a real problem with darkness. What triggered his condition? That's anybody's guess. If his parents turned out all the lights in his bedroom, he would become terrified. His parents tried many things, including reading him stories at night until he went to sleep. They finally found that a small nightlight did the trick.

Unfortunately, unlike most cases, this phobia never went away. He carried it into adulthood. When he drove at night, he always insisted on will-lit highways. This never became a real problem until he was married. Unfortunately his wife cannot sleep with the light on. The problem was solved using separate bedrooms.

*****

Nancy Carter was a young woman in her 20s. She was terrified of dark places, especially alleys. In New York there were plenty of those. Even being there with men she trusted, she refused to go into them.

Most people, men and women alike, will avoid alleys like that, unless necessary. Nancy was pulled into a dark alley one night, and brutally raped. She was in her early teens at this time. Up to that point, the dark hadn't bothered her. After that experience, she always left the nightlight on in her bedroom. She always avoided dark places. Under the circumstances, that was easy to understand. This was a phobia that stayed with her throughout her life. She had an understanding husband, who honored her wishes.

Most people do not like total darkness, except in bed. The fear of falling down unlit stairways and the like brings out our instinct for self-preservation. This is especially true for the older generation. A fall could be fatal or disable them for life.

Stories of monsters popping out from behind trees on dark city streets have been told to us since childhood. Most of us are not fond of being in that situation, however that would not be considered a phobia, only common sense.

Fear of heights

Many people are afraid of heights. When it becomes extreme, there's a name for it. Acrophobia, or fear of high places, is more common than one might think. It's easy to get dizzy looking down from a high building, especially those with a glass elevator. There are many degrees of this fear.

Robert Downing had this problem all his life. As a young boy he fell from a high tree branch breaking his arm. That was the last time he ever climbed anything. Because of this condition, his military career was confined to the United States, as an Army recruiter. The Army psychiatrist did him no good.

*****

Mary Borden was a woman in her late 20s. She had always been scared to death of anyplace over 8 feet off the ground. She could not comfortably ride an elevator. Unlike Mr. Downing, she had never fallen. What caused this fear with her could probably have been found in her childhood somewhere, but her therapist was never able to figure out the reason.

*****

Charles Wilson often marveled as he watched skyscrapers grow in New York City. He could never understand the Native-American construction workers with their ability to walk on narrow beams sixty stories and more off the ground.

The thought of going near the edge on the roof of a single building, would cause him cold sweats. He always felt his condition was probably the result of a fall from a hayloft in his grandfather's barn as a child. Although he barely had a memory of this happening, a psychologist friend of his brought it out into the open. This friend tried in vain for two years to get Charles away from these feelings of dread. This phobia stayed with Charles for life.

For elderly people the condition is understandable. Usually it's not the height, but the fear of falling down. Stairways are especially frightening to them, as this will often result in a fractured hip. But in their case this can hardly be considered a phobia, again, just common sense.

Fear of spiders

Arachnophobia is an intense fear of spiders. Most of us don't like them, even though the majorities are perfectly harmless. In the film industry, the tarantula is generally used to scare people. The reality is black widow spiders are dozens of times more dangerous. Contrary to common belief, if a tarantula is walking on your arm, for instance, it would be hard for it to bite you. Its venom is not that dangerous, except to other insects.

....

Luanne Martin was ten years old when she was out hiking with her parents in Missouri. While stopping for a breather, she was bitten by a brown recluse spider. These spiders are dangerous and that bite resulted in the loss of a kidney. She felt the effects of it for many years, and developed a hatred, and fear of spiders. She felt faint at the sight of a common household spider, called daddy long legs. This phobia stayed with her for life.

It's   *****

Richard Edson developed a fear of spiders, at age 6. Here again, it was from being bitten. He was playing outside near a woodpile. He saw a black spider walking across a piece of plywood and went over to investigate. He picked it up and was bitten. At his age he could've died from the bite. Luckily he let out a scream, and his mother came out and immediately drove him to an emergency room at the local hospital. He was barely conscious when she got him there.

At that point he developed and retained a fear of all spiders. This condition stayed with him for life. Although he realized not all spiders were dangerous, he still maintained a phobia about them and kept his distance.

José Lopez was walking down a path in his native South America. Passing under a tree branch he felt something drop onto his shoulder. Before he could stop it, the spider went to his neck where he felt a sharp sting. He brushed it off himself. Fortunately this was not the first time he had seen that species of spider. He had been at the zoo a week earlier and recognized it as a highly toxic banana spider.

He swiftly made his way to the highway and was able to get a ride to the closest hospital. He had told the driver of the car what it happened. He told the man who was a banana spider. It was fortunate he done that as he lost consciousness on the way. On ant venom saved his life.

*****

Insect-phobia

A condition related to arachnophobia is insect-phobia. It is an intense fear of insects of all types. Although it's common knowledge that we need these creatures, some people still fear them. Few of these present any danger to humans.

On a trip to the forests of Oregon, Brian Jenkins was stung by a fire ant. These creatures have an intense sting, although not dangerous unless stung by hordes of these. Brian, at age twelve, became terrified of any sort of insects. This was true especially of Bee's or any other type of insect with a sting. The sight of practically any type of insect would put him into a cold sweat. This phobia has stayed with him for most of his life.

....

Barbara-Ann was on the desert of Arizona when bitten by a bark scorpion. This type can be very dangerous. Her parents rushed her to the hospital in Tucson, where she was treated and released. She had intense breathing problems as well as excruciating pain. This resulted in an intense fear of all arachnids. This phobia stayed with her until she received professional help. She still doesn't like scorpions.

The bark scorpion is at the top of the list for fatalities from scorpion stings in the United States. Scorpions are nocturnal and predatory. The

Tilson at the end of the tail contains the stinger. Scorpions do have venom but, out of over seventeen hundred species, only about twenty worldwide, are dangerous or fatal to humans.

Bart Anderson had a similar thing happen to him. He was rooting around a woodpile on his grandfather's farm in Cochise Arizona. It was a chilly evening, and getting dark. He got out to get firewood and was looking for a decent sized log. He found a few and was carrying them back to the farmhouse when he felt a sharp sting on his arm. This caused him to drop the logs. Looking down he saw a scorpion scampering away from the wood. He didn't think much about it until he got the logs in the house. Then his arm began to swell with pain. His grandfather drove him to a local medical center. He described the scorpion to the nurse and she bought a book with several pictures and asked if he could identify it. It was not a dangerous variety however quite capable of being painful, as Bart found out.

Fear of snakes

A common phobia shared by a large part of the population is Ophidio-phobia. This is an intense fear of snakes. It becomes a phobia when the mere sight of any type of snake can cause hypertension and cold sweats. Of all the species of snakes, only a few are poisonous. Constructors can kill by wrapping themselves around prey. For the most part, snakes are not dangerous to people.

Rattlesnakes, which are the most common venomous snake, can kill a human, but seldom do. Three out of four bites by a rattlesnake are dry bites. This means they will bite but do not inject venom. Baby rattlesnakes on the other hand are the most dangerous. When they inject their venom they don't know when to stop. Their venom is as lethal as the full-grown snakes. The cottonmouth, found mostly in the southeast United States, is dangerous to humans. On the West Coast the diamondback and Red Mountain Rattler, are the most common.

Snakes will not attack humans, although some cases of cobras attacking humans in areas of Africa and India have been documented. An attack and bite from the King cobra will often kill its prey immediately. This is true also of the black mamba, and the brown snake, found mostly in Australia. These can kill a human within minutes.

Danny Peterson's father was a herpetologist at the zoo in Griffith Park in Los Angeles. His father, Sam, milked rattlesnakes for their venom. This venom was used throughout the world in hospitals and scientific laboratories. Venom is used for a cure in snakebite cases.

Danny's father moved to San Diego in nineteen forty-one. At that time he married Elva, who had been his secretary at the zoo. When Danny was five years old he was playing with one of his father's King snakes'. One of them bit him on the finger. When he lifted his hand the snake hung on. This caused a lifetime fear of snakes. Living on a hill full of snakes caused him great consternation. This experience left him feeling a great fear of snakes for the rest of his life.

*****

Annie Woodward, living in Florida near the Everglades, had been around snakes most of her life. She developed a phobia against them when bitten by a cottonmouth at the age of seven. Never losing consciousness, she was rushed to the hospital and treated for the bite. From that day forward she had an intense fear of snakes and lizards. This fear became so intense that her parents had to move to an area free of snakes.

Snakes, even venomous ones, are more afraid of humans than we are of them. Very few snakes will attack a human being. Although rare, an exception to this is the King cobra. A cobra is the snake of choice for snake charmers throughout the Middle East. The snake charmer charms the animal by the movements of his hands. It has a hypnotic effect on them. Snake charmers are seldom bitten when doing this. It's an art that's been around since the days of ancient Egypt and before.

The largest of all snakes in the world is the Anaconda. Like most cases, if it is cornered, it will fight back. It does this by wrapping itself around the body and strangling it. They've been known to bring down crocodiles and water buffalo. One of the largest of these snakes was, at 28 feet, the largest found. This author's brother, Steven, a park ranger was given the responsibility to acquire the animal for a New York zoo.

There is a superstition that if one kills and eats a large snake of this variety, they will gain supernatural powers. For this reason the Anaconda never made it to the United States. A root problem for many of us is the story of Adam and Eve. Eve is convinced by a viper to eat forbidden fruit, which she does. For that reason, God punishes all of us. Is it a fable? For sure, but it's ingrained a fear of snakes in most of us.

Fear of public speaking

Gloss phobia is an intense fear of speaking or performing in public. If a person is not used to it, almost anybody will feel uncomfortable. Some great performers, Maria callus, one of the great opera singers of our time, for example, would literally get sick before her performance. This is true of many musical artists even though they perform all the time.

As part of his work, John Hanson was called on to get up before an audience and make a presentation. He was told by his superiors to make a speech before doing this. He passed out on the way to the stage. Doctors could find no reason for this, but John knew the problem. He had never been able to give a talk in front of anybody.

As a child he was constantly being punished for talking. Over a few years he developed a phobia for speaking to any group, no matter the size. He would get physically ill over doing this.

In his late 30s, he joined a Toastmasters group. This nationwide organization, started by a man working for General Dynamics in San Diego, Derwood English, has helped many people to learn to speak in public. This did not cure John's problem, but certainly helped it.

René Solis, a cellist with a major symphony, had no problem performing in public, until she was called upon to do a speech for a group of contributors to the orchestra. For two weeks she was in cold sweats constantly. She was frequently vomiting the day of the speech. For that reason she had to decline. Although she was used to performing with a large group, she was too self-conscious to speak that night. Even several consultations with a psychiatrist, did not make her problem go away.

Elmer Addison had no idea public speaking could be any problem for him. He was used to getting out with friends and talking to them even in crowded places. It never dawned on him that in front of an audience, he would be the center of attention. His hobby is restoring antique cars and was asked by a car club in Reno, Nevada to give a talk. He freely volunteered and looked forward to the experience. That is until he began walking across the stage.

He got to the microphone, pulled out his notes and started to talk. After introducing himself his mind went completely blank. His mouth was dry and he was unable to speak. That wasn't bad enough. He could literally not move. One of the men walked onto the stage and helped him off. Stage fright is not that uncommon. I have it myself.

Fear of thunder and lightning

Bronto-phobia is an intense fear of thunder and lightning. Although most of us do not like to be outdoors during it, some people get physically sick being indoors and listening to it. For that reason they choose to live in other areas not affected by it.

As a child, Sally-Ann did not understand where the noise and light came from. Her father instilled in her, a fear of it when he told her it was warning of the devil coming to visit her. Of course he was only joking with her, but at four years old, she didn't know it. Her father died shortly after her fifth birthday, but she never forgot his warning. It was a phobia that would cause her to get physically ill during rainy weather. Several sessions with a psychiatrist helped, but didn't completely cure her.   *****

Thomas Tamayo emigrated from Japan at the age of twelve. While riding a bicycle home during a lightning storm, he was struck by lightning. Almost killing him, it caused a phobia which lasted most of the rest of his life. It went on the wane, as he got into his 60s, but it was still there. Surprisingly enough, the rain never bothered him. However, the thunder and lightning was an entirely different story.

Fear of technology

Many people do not like our modern world and would like to go back a hundred or more years. A more up-to-date version of this is called technophobia. It's a fear of computers, radio and television, machinery and what they've done to the modern world. Many people of the older generations don't use computers, however they don't hate them. A true technophobia, if given the choice, would eradicate everything modern from the planet.

The British luddites were a large group of people that tried to stop technology. Their feelings were that many people, dating back to the industrial revolution, had lost their jobs to technology. Workers in factories, farmworkers, workers in the construction trades, and many other jobs over the years, have gone by the wayside due to new technologies coming every day. So many jobs these days are computerized, and the trend is growing. Most people want progress, some just don't want it going on too long.

It seems the more advanced the technology, the more a lot of people fear for their livelihoods. This fear has led to a lot of problems. People use the environment as an excuse to pose demonstrations against many forms of the modern world. Most notably is the automobile industry. Like it or not the masses are not going back to horses. New technologies, such as electric cars or those running on hydrogen, and solar power may limit the use of petroleum-based products, but they'll still be needed.

A prime example of people wanting nothing to do with technology is a religious sect in Pennsylvania known as the Amish. They use horses and buggies for transportation, and gas and candle lighting inside their homes. For the most part, they want nothing of the modern world.

The men do the manual work of feeding and keeping the animals, as well as farming. What they don't use for themselves is sold at markets in town. Their women are strict housekeepers and help family finances by quilting blankets, doing artwork, making their own clothes and selling those products they don't use.

Gerald and Lucy Porter own a farm in rural Pennsylvania. They were born and raised in the Amish-Mennonite environment. They were taught to believe that all technology is against the will of God. They are basically Christian and attend baptismal services as well. They support themselves farming and selling their crops in towns, or barter goods with their neighbors. Lucy spends most of her time keeping their home up and doing sewing and crocheting.

They have deep religious convictions. Like most of the Amish, their education stopped at the eighth grade. They were home educated by their parents and brought up to believe what their parents told them.

They both have ingrained an intense dislike for any modern technology, and like their neighbors, get around in a horse and buggy. They have nine children, who they homeschooled and put to work in the fields afterwards.

This way of life has been going on for generations. Orchung is the official set of rules for the church, which the Amish people are required to follow. Founded in Switzerland in the nineteenth century, the religion preaches that God does not want progress. The Amish people migrated to areas of Pennsylvania, Indiana and Canada. How long the younger generations are going to follow their parent's example is hard to say.

Technology has been a boon to civilization. Like it or not, the human race has advanced more in the last two hundred years, than in all of history. There will always be detractors to anything new or not understood. It's the human psyche.

Fear of rape

Virgnitiphobia is a condition prevalent in many men and women alike. The fear of being raped only becomes a phobia when it's all one can think about. Reasons for this vary, but in most cases it can go back to childhood. Many women that have had this happen to them in their teens and 20s, develop a fear of men (Arrhenphobia). In most cases this condition will cause many problems for a woman, but can be helped up to a point, by psychiatry.

A Portland psychiatrist had a patient, Geraldine who had an intense fear of being around men. She was an attractive twenty-one-year-old woman. This condition had caused her problems for many years. Her father died when she was five years old. Her mother remarried a man with an older son.

A few sessions with her psychiatrist, as well as a hypnotist, and she was able to restore a hidden memory. Her stepbrother had come into her room when she was seven years old. He brutally raped her, and threatened to kill her if she ever said anything about it. She had completely blacked out all memories of this.

The statute of limitations had run out so he could not be tried for his crime, however, he was forced to leave town with his wife, when this knowledge was brought to the forefront.

*****

Geraldine Martinique began seeing a psychiatrist for a weight problem. The doctor brought in a hypnotist from his office. Although she had never been sexually molested as a child, the hypnotist had her convinced she had. The blame fell on her father, a Baptist minister. Her father was innocent of this, but had a hard time convincing his daughter he'd never laid a hand on her. The hypnotist was later found to have given her a posthypnotic suggestion blaming her father. Doctor Williams already escaped the authority of another state for doing this. He was prosecuted, and lost his license to practice.

Rape in men is seldom prosecuted, especially if done by a woman. Although unusual, it does happen. In most cases, however, a man can be attacked. This often happens when coming out of a bar. Another man in the bar may take notice and for one reason or another, think his victim desires him sexually.

In most cases, the act will be performed when the victim is still a child. A memory like this in women can ruin their life and in some cases cause the man to become a felon.

Jeremy Downs was a young man of seventeen. He got into trouble with the law when he robbed a gas station. He was tried as an adult and sentenced to ten years in the state prison. Being a young man, he was raped by an older man sharing his cell. Although unusual, it happens.

Although the two were separated, this traumatic event scored him for life. Being paroled after seven years, he found life on the outside hard and unfortunately was back in prison within a year. One of the prisoners, attempted to solicit Jeremy. In a fit of rage, he beat the man to death. Jeremy died in prison at age 60.

The act of rape is as old as history itself. In our ancestors, dating back to the dawn of history, rape against women was common among men. Perhaps it was a desire to propagate the human race, but more likely for the sheer pleasure of it. Unfortunately, memory is usually fixed by something we'd rather forget.

Fear of illness

Path phobia is inherent in all of us, up to a point. Often classed as a hypochondriac, people with this disorder have an intense fear of disease. Sometimes this becomes an obsession.

Nadine Damon has a severe form of this problem. Staying in most of the time, when she does go out, she's always careful about whom she comes in contact with. If anybody around her so much as coughs, the surgical mask comes out of her purse immediately. At times this becomes a real problem for her.

Being young and attractive, she is often asked out but declines. She refuses to be anywhere she can be in contact with germs. This phobia was ruining her life. When she finally realized this, she contacted her doctor who in turn recommended a psychiatrist. He was able to get her over her problem and she began to have a reasonably normal life.

*****

Sal Rickman is a journalist. He developed path phobia when working overseas in Cambodia. Many of the diseases there are fatal. He came in contact with a form of malaria, which almost cost him his life. From that time, any form of any disease terrified him. On returning to the

United States, he continued his journalism career, but worked out of his home.

He was afraid to come in contact with anybody for fear of catching something. Even psychiatry didn't work for him. He was convinced for life, that any kind of disease would kill him.

*****

Gloria Freeman developed this fear as a child in the early twentieth century. She had witnessed the death of her mother from a flu virus. I younger sibling died two weeks later. Gloria became intensely afraid of disease, and would only leave her home wearing a mask. Her family was aware of her problem and helped her and every way possible.

Ironically, she contracted the flu virus is in an open market after removing her mask to smell a head of cabbage. She died a month later.

The fear of coming in contact with disease is inherent in all humans. Being intelligent, we understand the ramifications of being sick, or catching something that will make us sick. Colds and flu viruses are the most common causes. Most potentially fatal diseases are curable. Nobody likes to be sick, however in most cases we get well again.

Fear of ancestry

A problem that has affected several people over many years is Patroio-phobia. It is an intense fear of ancestry. People with this phobia constantly use genealogy to satisfy themselves. Some of us are curious about our ancestors but curiosity is as far as it goes. In some cases it's used by the medical profession to determine if we are predestined to certain disease which can be passed on from generation to generation. With some, it becomes an obsession.

In his younger life, Robert Wilson had been told stories of his family's past. His parents died in an automobile accident. He went to live with his grandparents in another state. He had been told his great-great-grandfather was one of the heroes of the Civil War. As much as he tried, he could never substantiate this.

Other stories of family heroism, especially war stories, became a mystery as well. Over years of time, he was obsessed with finding the truth. His grandparents always insisted the stories were true. When investigating tales of royalty, he hit a dead end as well. Finding the truth became his life's work.

To most of us genealogy is more a curiosity than an obsession. Why kids are lied to may be an attempt to give them a feeling of self-worth.

In other cases they may just be considered white lies, the kids growing up, believe. In some cases, like Robert Wilson's, it may become a lifetime obsession to find the truth. As Senator Douglas once remarked, "it's easier to build strong children, than to repair broken men."

As a teen, Mary Woods was told she was descended from royalty. She spent years try to substantiate this. Unfortunately, at that time computers were toys and information on genealogy was not available to her. After awakening from a nightmare, one morning, she began having fears of a descendant of a victim of a former ruler's cruelty come after her. She realized that fear was ridiculous, but couldn't seem to shake it. A couple of weeks with a therapist solved the problem. At eighteen, she is now free of her anxiety.

Fear of dreams

Oneirophobia is a fear of dreams. Most of us have had dreams and many nightmares since we were children. If given the time we can usually figure out where they came from, if indeed we can even remember them. Dreams are merely a cleansing of the mind. Some people take them seriously, as mentioned in the previous chapter.

In Janice Allen's case, she felt her dreams had deep meanings to them. This may have been the case, however she thought her dreams could foretell the future. She soon began to become neurotic over them. Regardless of what she believed, family members would often try to calm her down by explaining to her that dreams do not foretell the future. This phobia started when she was a child of six. Like most children her age, she had dreams of monsters attacking her while she was in bed.

Her mother would often come into her bedroom and comfort her when she heard Janice screaming for help. Not too uncommon, however Janice sincerely believed her dreams were telling the future.

Through her teens and into her early 20s, many of the day-to-day decisions she made were based on what she could remember of dreams she had. Most of these dreams turned out to be figments of her imagination. The few that bore fruit caused her to believe her dreams could foretell future events. It took psychiatry to dispel these theories. She is now happily married, and still dreams on a regular basis. Now she will often lie in bed and figure out where these dreams came from. In most cases she realizes parts of the dreams are manufactured by her, in the twilight before she awakens.

*****

Willie Anderson suffered from these delusions as well. As a lieutenant in the Army, he would often make military decisions based on his dreams. This could become very dangerous for the men under his command.

In one instance he'd ordered his men to concentrate their fire on a hill near a village. The danger was insurgents driving out of the village. It was later learned nobody was on the hill. Luckily this didn't cost any lives. He was still convinced his dreams could foretell future events. That feeling was strengthened when enemy forces did come over that hill a few days later.

It is not uncommon for dreams to come true. Many of these can be from fear or anticipation of events that come into our lives. Most psychiatrists and psychologists put a lot of stock into what their patients say when talking about their dreams. They realize that dreams come out of one's subconscious. This can be an invaluable help to their patients as well as a tool to determining whatever problems they may have.

In closing this portion, I do have a bizarre story to tell. As strange as it sounds, it is true.

My mother had four dreams in her lifetime which stood out from all the rest. She dreamt a black gloved hand came down onto her bed and went around her throat. The next day her father was forced off the highway by a Greyhound bus. The new nineteen twenty-eight Chrysler he was driving went down a hill and into a tree. The steering wheel went through his chest, killing him immediately.

The second of these dreams came a few years later, the night before she was going to ride on a plane owned by a friend of hers, she dreamt of the black glove. She called him and canceled. That afternoon the plane crashed killing her friend and his companions.

The third of these was a similar story. Mom was scheduled to come down from Canada on a train however the dream caused her to turn the ticket in, hours before the train crashed, killing many of the people on board. The fourth and last time she had that dream was the night before my brother went to Vietnam. Needless to say, she was scared to death. My brother did go there, and came home safely two years later.

Dreams do come from our sub-conscious. This we know to be a fact. However, strange things do happen.

Selma Meyer migrated to the United States with her family during the Second World War. She was eighteen years of age and Jewish. They had managed to escape before the crackdown. Her father was a well-known biologist. Because of this, they were allowed into the United States, unlike many of their brethren on the same ship.

For months she could not shake the feeling of impending doom. This feeling was heightened during nightmares she experienced every time she fell asleep. This got to the point where she was afraid to sleep at night.

She told her father about this and he immediately contacted one of the men in his lab who is a psychologist. Her dad set up an appointment for his daughter to see Doctor George Pearson. After two weeks of intense treatment, her anxieties and dreams disappeared. Will

Fear of bondage

Merinthophobia is the fear of being tied up or bound by any type of restraint. Although it's possible this may start much younger, it's usually not considered a phobia until the teen years.

Martin Alexander at age 5 was bound with rope by his parents and thrown into a closet. They dumped gasoline on the floor, set a fire and walked out of the house. It's amazing he was still alive when paramedics found him. He had severe burns on his whole body. His face and head was scorched and all his hair burned off. At the hospital, physicians worked on him for over six hours. He suffered through skin grafts for the next several months. He was made a ward of the state and his parents were tried and convicted of attempted murder and insurance fraud.

From that time on, Martin was deathly afraid of any type of restraint anywhere on his body. For some strange reason, fires didn't bother him. Although seeing a psychiatrist on several occasions, he never got over his aversion to having restraints on him.

*****

Laura Mather also fell into this category. It didn't take long for her psychiatrist to diagnose her problem. Laura was a pretty girl in her early

20s. In her early teens, she had been bound and gagged before being brutally raped by her step grandfather.

Shortly after moving into the house, he was asked to take care of her. He did that all right. Laura's parents didn't believe her when they got back, however because of this accusation, the grandfather was asked to leave because Laura could not be in the same room with him.

Being raped at this age by a family member, does not usually involve being tied up first. Most rape cases are usually on young to middle-age women at the hands of an older man. Most of these cases do involve bondage, and sometimes lead to a phobia which can leave them scarred for a long period to come.

Bill Carter was unmarried and a ranking member of the Chicago mob. Police had been called out to a gangland hit. Members of the organization felt Carter had something to do with it. In gangland style, he was taken out to the water. He was bound, gagged, and thrown off a pier in Atlantic City. The mob felt it had done itself a favor. Nothing could've been further from the truth. Bill had the good luck to be seen by somebody under that pier, and pulled to safety. He was incensed at what had happened to him and gave the FBI what they needed to put the Atlantic mob behind bars. In a plea agreement he was given a new identity and residence in a small Midwestern town.

Although he had always had a bit of an aversion to being handcuffed, he was now scared to death of any type of restraint, whether being handcuffed, bound by rope, or gagged. This straightened Bill Carter out in a hurry. At age 35, he met and fell in love with a young woman he had met one morning during breakfast at a local café. He now lives happily with her and has fathered two children. Few men like him have a happy ending.

*****

Hortense Murphy was a flapper during the 20s era. She enjoyed trips to the dance halls where she met many available men. Unfortunately, she was attracted to the bad boys. Because ethics at that time did not encourage young women taking men home with them, she never did.

Mickey Carmel came into her life and was soon the exception to that rule. Unfortunately, their first date didn't go well. He bound and gagged her, beat her then raped her. She called police, but never returned to the club. She was deathly afraid of any type of rope or gag after that experience.

Fear of horses

Hippo phobia; no this is not the fear of hippos. It's actually the fear of being around horses. Usually from childhood experiences.

Mary Jane, like many girls in their early teens had a love and fascination with horseback riding. One of her uncles gave her a horse on her fifteenth birthday. She loved and cared for this animal for the next couple of years. She was out riding scout one afternoon. Coming upon a rattlesnake in the bush, scout reared up on his hind legs throwing Mary Jane off him and into unconsciousness.

Feeling betrayed by scout, not realizing why he had done this, she never rode him again. Her aversion quickly grew to being around any horse, or even the smell of one. In most cases this is the reason for the phobia.

*****

Johnny Larson was never thrown from a horse. His phobia came from his father who had, on several occasions, told him stories of wild horses being tamed by Indians and later being killed by them when their horse attacked them. Although the stories were a bit outrageous, Johnny took them to heart. It was so bad; up until he was in his 20s, he could not even stand the sight of a horse. He was given psychiatric care and within six months, the aversion was gone. John Larson is now in his 50s. His psychosis has never returned.

Marne Weber was the daughter of horse rancher in Los Angeles. He worked on the ranch belonging to Claude Henderson (my grandfather).

Her father, Mike, was breaking a horse when it reared up and came down on top of him, breaking his back and almost killing him. Up to that point she loved being around the animals. She saw her mother nurse her dad back to health over a five-year period. From that time on she not only feared them, but hated them as well.

She met her husband to be at their parents' home on the ranch. He was one of the hands hired to care for the horses. She didn't want a repeat performance of her father's accident, but on the other hand love does funny things to a person. She had insisted that Mr. Henderson erected a fence around the house horse could not go over or through. Over a period of time her phobia lessened as her husband talked her into going into a stable on occasion. Over time she was able to pet a horse and later open the stall.

Although these were great breakthroughs for her, she was never able to lead or ride a horse again.

Fear of rooms

Koinoniphobia is a term given to the fear of being in certain rooms. It has nothing to do with claustrophobia. In most of these cases the fear stems from the death of a loved one in that room.

One such case was Mary Ellen Schubert. At age 70, she lost her husband of fifty-two years to cancer. He died in their bed at the age of seventy-two. Although family members had tried talking to her, she never stepped in that room again. She is now eighty years old, and the room is just as it was left after paramedics took her husband away.

Upon his parent's death, Scott Myers inherited a large rural home. There was a room of their home, where Scott had many undeserved whippings as a child. One would think his mother would put a stop to these, but she had a few of them herself. Her husband was a tyrant, of that there was no question. He was found dead from a two-story drop, in his 50s. The police could find no evidence of foul play; however they felt he was pushed. The case was ruled an accident. His mother passed away ten years later, of a heart attack.

The room remained off-limits to Scott. Because of his aversion he sold the house a few years after his mother's death, never having stepped in the room again. To this day he has never felt that problem with any other room.

A bizarre story came when Linda Sue Bailey inherited her sister's home after she died of a heart attack. The upstairs bedroom where her sister had passed away months before became a curiosity. One evening shortly after moving into the home, Linda Sue went upstairs to go through her sisters effects.

A cold chill came over her as she sat on the edge of the bed rummaging through one of the dresser drawers she had pulled out and brought over. As she turned around, she swears her sister was standing there, not saying anything. Linda Sue screamed, and the apparition went away. She locked the door to the room, and never stepped foot in it again.

Similar cases to hers have been documented throughout history. In certain Victorian mansions turned bed-and-breakfast, in the eastern part of the United States, have had claims of non-relatives seeing apparitions in certain rooms of the house. If these apparitions are projected by somebody living in the house to create advertisement for their business, may never be known.

Fear of ridicule

Kainotophobia is a fear of ridicule. True, most people don't like being ridiculed. However, in more severe cases the person affected will go out of their way to see that doesn't happen. Consequently they never seem to get anywhere. Eric Franklin was one such example.

Eric was a handsome young man, twenty years of age. As far back as he can remember, his parents teased him all the time. He was constantly being told that he couldn't do anything. Thus the seeds were planted in his mind, that he could do nothing right. He was afraid of being scorned, so kept to himself. He didn't have much of a social life, if any. As he got older, the condition worsened.

He stayed away from the opposite sex, fearing he could never live up to their expectations. He had a go-nowhere job as an analyst in an insurance company. The few times his superiors said anything against his work, he would have to leave, feeling physically ill. They soon learned to leave him alone.

At age 22 a lucky break came to him. One of the girls in the secretarial pool had an eye on him. She realized he was painfully shy. She approached him on a Friday evening as he was getting onto an elevator to go home.

She rode down the fifteen floors with him to the lobby. During that time she asked if he would like to come to dinner at her place. This was a whole different deal for Eric. Nothing like this had ever happened to him before. He knew he wanted to do it, but couldn't.

A week later on Friday night, there was a repeat performance of the last time. This time she made it sound like a favor. She wanted him to come over and help her on some things she was working on. That Friday night he reluctantly drove to her home. By the time he got to her door he was sweating profusely on the forehead as well as his hands. Bethany had been careful the way she dressed. She was neat, but not flashy. Eric was dressed in slacks and a sport coat. She was slowly able to calm his nerves. She had fixed them a nice meal.

After the dinner was over, she asked that he help her with the dishes. She did this to help calm him further. It did the job. By evening's end, he was feeling much better. He could not quite bring himself to give her a goodnight kiss, but felt a handshake would do. She let that one go for now. She decided not to give up on this guy.

At the office and elsewhere he remained painfully shy. He did begin to come out of his shell after a couple months with Bethany. He was beginning to feel good about himself, which was a whole new thing for him. After a few more months with some therapy set up by Bethany, he began feeling comfortable around everybody.

As a footnote, he and Bethany married and have a child and another on the way. Eric was careful to see to it his children were never ridiculed and would have a good self-image.

*****

Barbara was a woman of thirty. Her mother always rode her as a child. She wanted marriage, but was painfully shy. Subconsciously, she gained weight and let herself go in many other ways. She worked as a secretary in a mechanics garage.

Although college-educated, she never felt she could measure up to anything much better than she had. Her employer, Barry Fielding, could see through her appearance. After several months, he asked her to join him at a self-help seminar. This experience completely changed her life. She joined Weight Watchers and was soon able to exercise. Her next step was a gym membership.

She and Barry begin to see each other after work on a regular basis. Soon Barbara had everything she wanted. She had lost close to 100 pounds, had her hair styled, and bought some decent clothes.

She and Barry went their separate ways. In the meantime she had gained the confidence to go out on her own. She was able to get a bank loan to finance a business of her own and use the knowledge she had gained at the University. She now has a successful limousine business.

Scott Wilder developed this phobia over time. He'd worked his way up to the presidency of a large produce company. Their products were shipped nationwide. When he was blamed for the recall of tons of lettuce, he began a downward spiral of self-worth. Because of this, over the next couple years he had five demotions. The more this went on, the worse the phobia became. When being assigned to the floor, he quit the company. His feelings of self-worth deepened as he sat in his living room day after day. He finally decided to do something about it and sought professional help. He is now on the road to recovery and working his way up the ladder in another company.

A good self-image is important to everybody no matter what walk of life. It's unfortunate some people don't have the parenting skills to see to it that their children are happy in life. That's one reason psychologists and psychiatrists stay busy.

*****

Fear of doctors

Latophobia is the fear of doctors, or going to see a doctor. This is a phobia that can be fatal. Many cases of terminal illness have occurred, due to this problem.

Marlene Franks had not been to a doctor since age 6. Her mother died shortly after. She had an incurable form of leukemia. Marlene's father left her in the care of his sister. Her aunt constantly berated the doctor's ability to help her sister in law. These words stuck with Marlene. She vowed to never step foot in a doctor's office.

Through marriage and two children, she kept this vow. Her children were both delivered at home by a midwife. Her husband paid little attention to this, figuring her health was her business. All was well until Marlene hit age forty-five. She began feeling weak, but refused to go to the hospital. It was found, too late, that she had lung cancer. At that point there was little doctors could do to save her life. Had she had regular checkups, certain medications and radiation could've saved her life. She died three months later.

*****

Whelan Bailey had a similar case to Marlene. He too lost his mother at an early age. He blamed the doctors for his loss, and refused to see another for many years. He developed epilepsy in his late teen years. He had to see a neurologist, as his first seizure was in a public park late one afternoon. He had a grand mal seizure which left him in spastic throes for over an hour.

He awoke in the hospital. When he came out of it, he was deathly sick. As a result, doctors left him in the hospital overnight. Awaking the next morning, he was on top of the world. He realized in this condition, he would have to get over his phobia against doctors. With a little professional help, he was able to do this. He was put on Dilantin, and remained seizure free.

Nobody likes to be in need of a doctor or hospital, but when we need them, they're a godsend. They are probably the best educated of all professionals, having to go through years of college and medical school. In this day and age, they all have their specialties, which is certainly beneficial to their patients in most cases.

*****

Fear of guns

Hopliaphobia is an intense fear of firearms. Somebody with this disorder becomes clammy with sweat by the sight of a gun. It doesn't necessarily have to be pointed at them.

Mario Macias, at age 5, was shot by his brother with a BB gun. Although not hurt, the impact of the shell mentally scarred him for life. From that point on, he had an intense fear of any type of firearm, whether pistol or rifle. His father, being a security guard, kept a pistol in a locked gun cabinet, which had a glass face. The site of the cabinet could cause him to get physically ill.

His brother, Carlos, five years his senior, trying to show off took a key from the shelf, and opened the Cabinet. He waved the pistol at Mario. His brother then began waving the gun around. The gun discharged hitting Carlos in the chest. He was taken to the emergency room, but died in transport. The fear of guns became a phobia, from which Mario never recovered.

*****

Mary Lee Green worked at her father's gun shop. She and her fiancé, who managed the gun shop, were out on a pistol range. The gun her fiancé was using failed to release. For some unknown reason, he hit the gun on a steel plate. The gun went off; the bullet hit the steel plate and ricocheted, hitting him in the head. He died immediately.

From that moment on, Mary Lee had an intense hatred and fear of any type of firearm. She had to leave her father's shop and find another job. To this day the sight of a gun of any kind will make her sick to her stomach.

John West Moreland had a fear of guns. This fear was probably more from the noise they made. At eight years old he was at a firing range with his dad. Unknown to his father, John had walked up to him and put his head on his dad's arm, just as he pulled the trigger.

This act caused him to lose his hearing in his one year. From that time on he was afraid to be anywhere around a gun or rifle.

In most cases, a person with this condition had a childhood trauma of one sort or another. Whether witnessing a relative or friend being shot, or being shot themselves is usually the cause for this fear.

In many cases, a well-intentioned father who tells his son or daughter of imaginary tales of people being shot can lead to this problem. This is especially true if the story is about a family member or friend, regardless of what the cause of their death.

Fear of fog

Homichiophobia is the intense fear of fog. How this condition comes to be is hard to explain. People with a condition like this will not venture outside on a foggy night.

As with most phobias, Charlie Daniels developed a fear of fog as a child. On a very foggy night, his family was coming home from church. His mother was riding outside the car on the running board, giving her husband directions. Coming around the corner, the car hit a deer crossing the road. The animal was killed in the impact which threw his mother off the car, severely injuring her. This incident scarred seven year old Daniel for life. Within a short time his dislike of foggy weather became a phobia. By the time he was ten, he couldn't even walk outside on a foggy night. Now at age 70, the event on that foggy night has caused his fear of fog which has lasted for life.

*****

Susan Edwards's fear of fog began as a young child when her father would always preface his mystery and horror stories to her with being in the fog. In those cases someone was always being shot to death or stabbed on a foggy night. For some reason, her father's sudden death from a heart attack caused her an intense fear of foggy nights. It took psychiatric sessions to ease her fears. To this day she will not drive in the fog.

Carolyn Butterfield could trace her phobia to an occurrence twenty years before when the headlights of another car came towards her on a foggy night. She could not be sure who was in the wrong lane, as the white line on the road was invisible to her and probably the other driver as well. She cut her car sharply to the right going off the road and stopping just short of a 200 foot drop, saving her life. She was unaware of the highway curve in front of her. That was the last time she ever ventured out of her home, for any reason, on a foggy night.

The phobia stayed with her for life.

In most mystery or horror stories, intense fog plays a strong role in the plot of the book or movie. In most instances a bad man or monster emerges from the fog to do bodily harm to somebody. It's easy to understand a person's desire to stay inside on nights like this. Not being able to isolate danger before it's too late is a fear most of us share. Besides limited vision, foggy nights are often cold, and a nice warm fireplace seems like a more sensible alternative.

Fear of losing

Kakorrhaphiophobia is an intense fear of losing. Any type of failure or defeat can cause the sufferer intense anxiety. Most people with this phobia are a "type A" personality.

Vernon Dyson was such a man. If he couldn't be the best at anything, he would refuse to even try. He would spend hours practicing anything that involved competitors. His phobia involved sports primarily. In running he would have to be the first to cross the finish line. In wrestling he would always pin his opponent, only being absolutely sure he could. In the game of chess he only played to the top of his level.

His desire to be the best at everything he did caused a few problems with his acquaintances. Many got to the point where they didn't even like to be around him. This phobia did tend to attract the ladies. His wife was docile, and pretty much gave him his way.

*****

Linda Sue Motley was also a "type A" personality. She was a marathon runner and methodically, practiced daily. She built up her body to the point where she could out-run anybody competing with her. In her personal life, her husband was also "type A". This got to be such a problem, that they soon divorced. Both found a more suitable mate for themselves. The saying "opposites attract", is often true.

Wanting to do one's best at anything is not a bad thing by any means. When it becomes a phobia, it also becomes a problem. It's not easy being around somebody like that.

The desire to be a top salesman certainly has its advantages until it becomes a phobia to the point, that it's all the victim will think about. In most cases a sufferer will go to great lengths to stay on top. This is good until that person makes it his life ambition at the cost of anything else.

We've all heard the stories of the captains of industry. The Rockefellers, the Vanderbilt's, Carnegie, the Aston's and many more like them. Without the strong desire to be on top, many of their accomplishments would have never come to fruition. In these cases there is certainly a phobia, or strong desire to get to the top and stay there. It's been said until age 92, Rockefeller would still bend over to pick up a nickel off a sidewalk.

To some people money means everything. If that's worthwhile at the cost of family and friends is up to the individual.

*****

Fear of responsibility

Hypegiaphobia is a chronic fear of responsibility. Someone with this condition refuses to take charge of any activity. In a lot of cases a person suffering from this, refuses to even take care of a child, unless it's their own. The person with this disorder may have been shielded of responsibility of anything, especially by parents with means.

One such person was Deanna Geer. Until her marriage, her needs were fully taken care of. Getting out into the world as a responsible adult was a completely new experience for her, and one she didn't relish. Her refusal to take charge of anything soon became a phobia. It took many sessions with a psychiatrist for her to get over it.

*****

William Presley's father was a take charge type of guy. Unfortunately, William was scared to death of his father. Up until his late teens, he lived with his parents. His mother was docile, and pretty much insisted her husband rule the roost. Being closer to his mother, William took on this trait himself. Although well-educated, this problem caused him the inability to perform duties required of him. For this reason, his jobs required subserviently bending down to everybody else's needs.

In all too many cases, a failed marriage, or business venture can cause a person to shrink away from trying anything again.

This was the case with Frank Wright. He had begun building a small manufacturing firm as a young man. His business began to build and everything looked good for him. Unfortunately, he overextended his credit, causing the bank to foreclose on his business. Because of his long hours away from home, his marriage soon failed as well. Before long other things began to fall apart for him as well.

He developed a real fear of trying anything again. He looked at himself as a failure, got a mundane job, and stayed with it for a couple of years, before getting psychiatric help. After a couple of years he was able to overcome his anxieties. He is now running a small business and is happily married. He vows to never allow his business interests to take over his personal life.

Many people have problems adjusting to new jobs, and getting up the nerve to accomplish some things. In most cases, time is the best healer of this, however in certain others, it becomes impossible. In these cases psychiatric care should be considered.

Fear of dependence

Soteriophobia is a fear of being dependent on anything or anybody. This can come about in earlier years, however in most cases; it's in the twilight years. It's most common in retirement homes.

Beth Schubert was a woman in her 60s, living in a retirement community. Her neighbors all seemed to have people coming in to do just about everything for them. She was upset by this. She always swore that she'd rather be dead than be unable to do things for herself.

As time went on, this became a phobia which she could not seem to shake. In later years she moved into a retirement home. Her cooking and cleaning needs were taken care of by the management. Although she didn't like the arrangement, she found she could no longer take care of herself. This became a factor in a heart attack, resulting in her death.

*****

John Morrow had always had a take charge personality. From the time he was age 16, out on his own, after his parents death, he always took the responsibility for doing anything. People, trying to help him were often ignored. This trait became a phobia for him, especially after marriage. He was lucky that he had a wife that could tolerate this. She, in fact, was a bit dependent on him. They had a good marriage, which included three children.

After her death at age 85, John moved into a retirement home, not wanting to be dependent on his children. His traits were tolerated by the building's management. They gave John a part-time job in the maintenance department fixing electrical circuits, small plumbing jobs, and even some janitorial services as well. This allowed him to keep his independence which he treasured. He lived just shy of his ninety-ninth birthday.

Most people take the middle road on this. In some things we want to be independent, but in others may, on occasion need help. This is true of almost anything one wants to accomplish.

*****

Joni LeClaire was a young woman living just outside of Paris. Although married, she treasured her independence and would often take trips by herself. After the death of her husband at age 40, she never remarried, but continued her independent lifestyle. As she began to age, she saw many of her friends going into senior care homes. The idea of this terrified her, until it became a necessity. At age 85 she suffered a severe stroke and could no longer take care of herself.

Fear of radiation

Radio phobia is a fear of radiation or x-rays. This is not as uncommon as one may think. Many people fear x-rays and radiation as being carcinogenic.

A case, in point, was Tom Thomas. He was a pilot for TWA who flew the transcontinental routes from New York to London and others.

He came to San Diego to visit friends, including yours truly. On his way back to Kansas City he began feeling faint and contacted his doctor when getting home. He developed brain cancer, and died four months later. The airline swore his condition had nothing to do with his job. Many people in the medical field do not agree with that, probably because of the high incidence of cancer among cockpit personnel.

*****

Another case was Robert Cox. As an Air Force pilot, he flew the B-29s, which stayed in the air twenty-four hours a day. He died from leukemia. I attended his funeral just yesterday. In talking to a friend this morning, several of his colleagues, working below high tension utility lines, had died from cancers of the brain as well as in other areas of the body.

There have been several cases of people developing various sorts of cancers dealing with radiation and x-ray. An example was the boxes used several decades ago in shoe stores. People would get a kick (enjoyment) out of coming in a store, taking off her shoes and socks and putting them into the box which x-rayed them and showed them on the screen. These were used extensively, until they found a lot of cases of people developing cancers, especially in their feet and legs. The boxes were soon outlawed.

Today radiation is used to destroy cancer cells. It's a common treatment and one which I have just gone through. It is entirely painless, however not without consequences. I have been unable to eat anything solid because of a sore on my tongue since undergoing the therapies. On the good side, being a bit obese, I've lost 25 pounds. However, I don't recommend this as a means of dieting. Another result is constantly being tired. Thankfully, both of these conditions will go away in time. I'm now editing this book a month later, and the conditions have pretty well gone away.

John Burris had an intense fear of radiation, seeing his grandfather die from it. Being exposed to the atomic blasts in southern Nevada during the development of the atomic bomb, he was part of the Manhattan project. During intense illness, doctors wanted to do a chest x-ray. John absolutely refused. That decision almost cost him his life. It was found that he had pneumococcal pneumonia. As a result of improper treatment he was in the hospital for a month and could not work for ninety days afterward. Although he now tempers decisions on radiation treatments, with a little common sense, he still doesn't like undergoing them.

Billy Ray is no fan of radiation, watching his father slowly die after attempts to save his life. Radiation was used, as surgery would have been impossible. After he suffered a similar disease, doctors could not get him to allow radiation treatments. His doctors tried to explain to him that modern radiation techniques were not the same as when they were used on his father. He began getting weaker as time went on, finally allowing the treatment. By that time was too late to save him. An autopsy showed an earlier treatment of radiation would've saved his life. He was survived by his wife and two teenaged sons.

Radiation, as with many other treatments, can be dangerous unless they are harnessed. At one-time chemotherapy was more dangerous than the disease however; new techniques pinpoint the cells doctors wish to destroy. These techniques will improve to the point of eradicating cancer cells altogether.

Stealing things

Kleptomania is a condition which becomes a phobia after time. It's a condition in which the sufferer takes things, mainly out of stores, without paying for them. In the words of some great philosopher, 'when I have bouts of kleptomania, I take something for it.'

As a youngster, I accompanied my mother into a lemon Grove grocery store. My father had asked that she pick up an avocado for him if she had any money left, which she didn't. I picked up an avocado, put in my jacket pocket, got in the car and went home. When we got there my mother was asked if she remembered the avocado. She said no; but I did. I proudly handed it to my dad. He didn't say a word, just put me back in the car and drove back to the store. I had to go back in the store and hand it to the manager. It was a lesson I never forgot and I can honestly say it was the last thing I ever took that didn't belong to me that I can remember.

Some kids aren't so lucky. One of my employees had a nephew raised to think stealing was okay. Things this guy would steal were often things he had no use for. He was truly a kleptomaniac. It got to the point where material companies insisted he stay in the truck.

Marceline Davis at age 13 started going into department stores with friends. She began going into dressing rooms and putting on underwear, and wearing it home. The girls began to have contests to see who could steal the most expensive items without being caught.

This phobia of hers got to the point where she would go into a gas station, pump gas and drive off without paying for it. She went a little too far, stealing a diamond necklace, and wearing it out of the jewelry store. She was caught and given a years' probation. She was back in court a month later. This time it was a car, for which she was given a year in jail.

Some people get a perverse pleasure of seeing what they can get away with. Most of us do not, although the thought does cross our minds from time to time. I like to think most people are honest. A kleptomaniac cannot help himself. It's a disorder which has to be treated with psychotherapy.

*****

Fear of loud noise

Lygyrophobia is the fear of loud noises. It can be a key factor, especially if you're going deaf as a result.

Philip Crowley worked as a press operator in an aircraft factory. At one point he realized his hearing was being jeopardized. As time went on he began to lose his hearing. He began to develop a phobia, literally becoming sick from the noise. He quit the job and moved over to another quieter section of the plant. From that time on any loud noise, even a car radio would have a negative effect on him. This condition stayed with him for life.   *****

Becky Ralston, as a young girl became frightened of the thunder in her hometown in the Midwest. Her father told her it was caused by the gods being angry. As time went on, she became more fearful of it and developed a phobia, which soon led to any loud noise. It got to the point where she could hardly tolerate the sound of a car door slamming, or a horn honking. After having children, it began getting worse. Their screaming often drove her into another room. Realizing she had to do something about this, she got professional help. That helped up to a point, but the phobia remained with her for life.

Praise and Flattery

A syc-o-phant is a pretty common condition until it becomes a phobia. People suffering from this condition flatter and praise people who hold high places in government or business, and those that are prominent or have great wealth.

In almost all cases this is an attempt to gain wealth or other favors. It is most common in government offices where people are trying to attain recognition and promotion.

Janice Brewer worked as a file clerk for the Department of Motor Vehicles. Rather than going through regular channels, like diligence and hard work, she did it with flattery. She was constantly telling other personnel, especially those superior to her, how nice he or she looked or how she admired the way they did their jobs. This behavior was especially welcomed by men working there. She would be asked out for dinner on occasion, and in the weeks to come would be promoted.

There is a saying, "some people are promoted to positions above their level of incompetence." This is certainly true of many people working in government offices, whether local, state or federal. Some of these people, like Janice, do it through flattery or even sexual favors.

Jack Moreland was an actuary for an insurance company. He worked his way up the ladder through praise and flattery to his superiors. Many of his fellow employees could see right through this ploy. Flattery however, has a way of getting through to people, especially those of the female persuasion. Jack played on this and was able to increase his position and salary over a couple years' time. After five years with the firm, he is now the vice president and has his eyes on the presidency.

The saying, "flattery will get you nowhere", is a fallacy. It will get you everywhere, if it's done right.

*****

The most common use of flattery is between a man and woman getting to know one another. In a case like this, neither can do anything wrong. The man will often make complementary gestures toward just about anything involving a woman. These include, but are certainly not limited to, complementing her clothing, the perfume she's wearing, the necklace, earrings, wristwatch, her shoes, the list goes on. The woman on the other hand, will usually complement his smell, his manner of dress and his appearance in general, regardless of whether she likes it or not. After all she can always change it after they're married.

Profanity

A problem found mostly in construction trades, is yelling insults and swearing at people. It's not pleasant to be around. In most cases it may be considered a bad habit. In some people it becomes a phobia. There are some people in society who can't utter a sentence without using profanity. This can be a result of little or no education, but in some cases a lack of self-esteem. This condition can result in scorn from those around them.

Joe Tracy worked as a framer on a construction crew. The company he worked for specialized in tracts of homes. Nobody paid much attention to his language, as other people on the job followed suit. He was constantly swearing at coworkers as well as other trades. He would yell insults to those he felt weren't working hard enough, or doing things wrong. The fact he was guilty of this very thing, never bothered him.

He, like many of his coworkers, realized they had to watch their mouths when people, especially their bosses would occasionally come around. He was berated more than once for the language he used.

After work, when not too tired, some of the people he worked with would get together at the local bar for a drink. In here they tried to be careful of their language, sometimes without much success.

On more than one occasion they were asked to leave. He would often take this attitude home. His wife didn't appreciate these actions; however, she usually left him alone. After all he was the breadwinner and made a decent living for them and their two children. He began thinking twice about his language, when he noticed his kids beginning to use it as well. Although he became careful around his wife and kids, he still kept his bad habits while on the job.

*****

Not so prominent in women, some are still guilty of excessive use of profane language. Marilyn Watkins worked as a bartender. She was constantly exposed to bad language at work, as well as at home. She began getting into the habit of swearing at the kids and on occasion her husband. Working in the bar, her language was certainly unladylike. Some of the men were amused by it, but the majority didn't appreciate it. When bar revenues went down, she was warned by her employer to watch her mouth. She was dismissed when she told him to go to hell.

She was fired from many jobs for this reason. She realized her demeanor was the reason, but try as she may, she couldn't seem to clean it up. Her husband was the same way, so it didn't bother him.

Their kids began to pick up on it. Their parents began being a little more careful of what they said. In fits of anger on the part of both of them, these behaviors would often return.

As the children grew into adults, their parents couldn't understand why their children grew up using this kind of language. They would never admit to being the reason for it.

Geraldine Bernstein was not happy with her fiancé's language. This was especially embarrassing to her in social situations with friends present. Her parents were not used to hearing that type of language as well, and questioned her choice of men because of it. Being a young woman, her parents not approving of something was a sure way of getting her to do it. She thought once she and Dale were married she would be able to change his ways. Unfortunately, that doesn't always work out. He continued until their five-year-old child began using it as well. At that point he became a little more careful. The jury is still out on whether this is a phobia or not. If not, it certainly is a bad habit and one which needs to be broken.

Fear of cats

Ailurophobia is a fear many people, mostly women, have of cats. Some of these are a result of being allergic to their fur. In that case it's not considered a phobia, just common sense to stay away from them.

In other cases the phobia may have something to do with black cats, witches and Halloween. In the days of ancient Egypt, cats were considered sacred and, or holy. Statues and engravings of them grace the great pyramids of Cheops as well as many other religious sites.

When Connie was four years of age, she was horribly scratched by her family's cat when she began roughhousing with it. The antibiotics put on the scratches, by her mother, were extremely painful. Since that time she had been deathly afraid of cats and will often get physically ill if she's around them. It makes no difference what breed of cat it is. All of them have that effect on her.

As a mother of two, she has a hard time explaining to her kids why they can't have a house cat, like the neighbors children do.

Fear of dogs

Cynophobia is an intense fear of dogs. It's natural to be careful around dogs. Like most animals, they are unpredictable. To most dog owners, their pet is perfectly harmless and in many cases this can be true. But dogs have a sixth sense about them. Most dogs can quickly pick up on an intense fear of them.

A case in point was "Chinook". He was a Siberian husky which I personally owned. He was probably the most docile animal I was ever around, except when it came to cats, he didn't like them. As a puppy, my niece would tell him "I love you", when she fed him. At one point in time, the dog howled "I love you" back to her. A Siberian husky is a wolf. They don't bark, they howl.

Within a couple of years any time you held food over his head, he would start shaking his head back and forth and howl "I love you". Now how docile can you be?

One of our employees had a thirty-six-year-old son. The guy was scared to death of dogs. He came into our construction yard at one time with his father. He was perspiring and although I told him the dog was perfectly harmless, he began shaking. I got down off the scaffold trailer to tie the dog up. Before I could do that, Chinook came over and started nuzzling him. He wouldn't leave the poor guy alone. I had never seen him act that way. The dog certainly realized the guy feared him.

People should have a healthy respect for any animal, be it tame or wild. In our business, I did plaster repair work for the insurance companies in hundreds of homes for many years, many of them with loose dogs in the yard or in the house. I have never been bitten by a dog. They always barked at me, but that's as far as it went.

I've heard cases where if you're chased by a lion or a bear in the wild, if you turn around, raise your arms and run towards them, not showing fear, they will run away. You're welcome to try that if you want to, I don't think I could.

*****

Bobbi Feldman was a young woman of twenty-one. She had an intense fear of dogs since she was a child of four. This phobia was so bad; she refused to be anywhere near a dog, even if it was chained up. Most people probably don't feel comfortable around dogs they are not familiar with, however with Bobbi; it didn't matter whether or not she was familiar with the animal. In her case, at age 7, she was savagely attacked by a neighbor's pit bull, when she started roughhousing with him. Having twenty-five stitches in her arms and legs, she was in a lot of pain for several weeks. Scars still remind her of that horrible afternoon.

*****

Frank Pierson had the wrong type of job for a man with this condition. He was a mailman in Los Angeles, California. He always carried a can of mace with him. In many cases a dog will not recognize the person but the uniform. This can usually be traced back to an incident where the uniformed man kicked or mistreated the animal.

With Frank Pierson, that was the case. The former carrier on the route had kicked and used mace on several of the animals coming near him, as he put mail into the mailboxes. In most instances, the dog's owners had been told not to let the dog out of the yard. In one instance the carrier was bitten on the leg. For this, the dog was put down.

Although Frank had never mistreated any of the animals in any way, he brought animals to the end of their chain many times.

*****

Feel a need to

Need to lie

Psedomania is a pre-disposition to lie. Some people have this condition to the point where it becomes a psychosis. There are those totally incapable of telling the truth. There are many people who will say almost anything to get themselves out of a jam. Once a person has a reputation for lying, it's hard to believe anything they say. In many cases, relationships between married couples can be a lasting example.

Catherine Bailey was a young woman living by herself in a house in rural San Diego County. She started seeing a guy who claimed to be a CIA agent. He would often be gone long periods at a stretch and then come back to see her, spend a couple of days and then leave again.

Catherine always had a thing for people with authority of any sort. Richard Jennings filled that need for her. This on again, off again relationship went on for almost two years. Catherine met Tim Ralston at a social function where she volunteered for Meals on Wheels.

She began forgetting about Richard. He hadn't been around to see her for almost a month. While Catherine and Tim were having coffee at a local Starbucks, the subject of dating came up. Catherine wanted to be up front with Tim and told him of her relationship with Richard. As she talked, Tim began to shake his head. He then proceeded to tell her that if Richard was an agent for the CIA, he would certainly have never told her so. Catherine had wanted to believe everything Richard said, and never questioned his sincerity.

Tim was a private detective and told her he'd look into this government agent of hers. Tim found that the guy was an employee at a local men's store. The pictures he brought to the table a couple days later were hard for Catherine to believe. Richard was walking out of the house, carrying a child, followed by a woman doing the same. It seems Catherine wasn't the only one Richard had on a string. Tim made up a dossier of the women Richard was seen with and sent it to his wife. He could only imagine what happened after that.

Lies of this sort are not uncommon and it's a problem both sexes have to deal with. A case in point is Jennifer and Reed.

The two met at a local park in downtown Chicago. Jennifer was not a raving beauty but certainly noticeable. She was a bit of a flirt which didn't seem to bother Reed, in the beginning. Jennifer was seeing three other men at the time. How she managed to juggle all four is anybody's guess. She seemed to manage.

The relationship with Reed became physical after a couple of weeks had past. They were spending more and more time with each other, however Jennifer always insisted on leaving after a bout of lovemaking with him. Reed, being a bit naïve, thought Jennifer just wanted to get back home to sleep in her own bed. In truth, she would go to a local bar and pick up one of her boyfriends. This seemed to work out for a while.

It didn't take Reed long to figure out what was going on. He found that her love life is not the only thing she lied about. She had a reputation for being a chronic liar as well. He broke off the relationship with her, which didn't make her happy. She swore she would be true to him, he knew better. He knew he could not trust her and realized he would never be able to believe what she said.

Salesmen are not free of this habit. In many cases, somebody trying to sell you something will often say anything they have to, in order to make the sale. The problem with lying to people is trying to keep what you say straight in your mind. Once somebody is caught in a lie, they have a hard time digging themselves out.

One such case was Barry Moore. In the last ten years he had sold everything from used cars to toasters. His favorite ploy was to lie about competitors' products. This would often get him in trouble with management. Some of his bosses were unscrupulous and didn't care what he said as long as he made the sale. But legitimate businesses wouldn't hire him because of his reputation.

Being a habitual liar often got him in trouble with his personal life as well. He had been married three times, lying to each to get an affirmative answer when he asked the woman to marry him. In each case they wanted a husband, but they could not abide his lies. His reputation spread to the point where he had to move to five different states. The last move cost him his life, when he lied to an underworld boss.

Many people regard "little white lies" as being okay. In most cases this is to protect a person's feelings. The only requirement of that, becomes knowing where to draw the line.

*****

Creative writing

Writing stories, poems or books is creative and enjoyable for a lot of people. When it becomes an obsession, however, it is known as typo- mania. This compulsion has affected many people over the years, as far back as the dark ages, when books began to be written. In some cases people were paid by the word when ghost writing.

For one reason or other, a person with this obsession will usually work laboriously at night and often all night. In some cases the author may want to continue while an idea is fresh in his or her mind, but in obsessive people they may continue because of an overwhelming urge to work.

Carl Alston was one such person. He never knew when to quit. In his case when he ran out of ideas on one subject, he would start another book. This went on for years. He never got anything published, or finished for that matter. He just felt an all-consuming urge to continue. He seldom left his apartment and became a recluse. When the cleaning crew came in one day, he was found dead in his apartment, hunched over his desk at the typewriter.

Rita Davis had a similar problem. In her case she was **agoraphobic and refused to leave her apartment. She spent all her time at the** typewriter, cranking out newspaper stories for the local paper. She supported herself as a book editor during the day. When finished she would start her writing, often staying up all night in order to finish a chapter.

Ideas did not come to her easily, and most were pilfered from books she edited during the day. She was never chastised by authors of these novels as she never had her works published. She would sometimes pick up an idea from a delivery person, and often that idea would turn into a chapter, however she was at a loss to ever finish.

*****

Josh Spalding wanted to be an author. He did finish a mystery novel which took him two years to write. Rather than trying to get it published he spent the best part of ten years reading and rewriting it. He had a phobia which told him nothing but perfection could be acceptable. This was carried through in most other parts of his life as well. On several occasions, he took his story to other writers, to get some idea of how he was doing. He was told several times to get the book published, unfortunately, he is yet to do that.

Almost any past time or occupation can become obsessive. There are those who feel this is the only way they can succeed. When that's done at the cost of a normal life, it can be detrimental to one's health and even life.

Betty-Ann Thompson was a compulsive writer. Having a scientific mind, her attempts at writing mystery novels were quite a chore for her. It was hard for her to come up with ideas that weren't included in scientific journals. It took her five years to write the Great American novel, another three years to edit it and get it published. She was sure the book would make her famous and wealthy.

Even using a famous New York publishing house, this did not happen. The biggest problem, being a scientist, she wrote way over the average reader's head. When friends would call her, she often had to explain what was meant by some phrase in her book. She finally decided to go off on other endeavors.

There are a lot of books being published today. These usually fall into two categories, fiction and nonfiction. In both categories there are subcategories; these include scientific journals, biographies, autobiographies and trade publications in nonfiction. Categories in fiction include science fiction, mystery, romance, and in some cases fiction written as nonfiction. This is not considered a phobia, unless it consumes your life.

Poison compulsion

Toxiophobia is more a compulsion than a phobia. It usually involves someone who has a death wish and has a desire to drink poisonous compounds. In this type of case, it's not a death wish. A person suffering from it feels a need to push the boundaries and see how far they can go. In most cases it's the emergency room.

Paula Adams had this compulsion. She was a woman in her early 20s with everything to live for. She had a man who had asked for her hand in marriage. She tried on many occasions to stop this compulsion. These poisons ranged from ant poison to snake venom, which she procured from the refrigerators at the zoo where she worked. She had never gone far enough to let a poisonous snake bite her, but she thought of it from time to time.

She finally had a talk with her fiancé about this. He had the good sense to suggest she seek professional help. He was in love with her and certainly didn't want to lose her. They contacted a psychiatrist near her home. She saw him twice a week for six months. Her compulsion left her. She is now happily married with two children.

*****

Robert Ruggles was a college student at a university in Port Hueneme, Florida. As a younger man he often had an urge to taste various poisons to see if they were similar. He had the good sense after putting one of these on his tongue to immediately use a rinse.

As he grew older this obsession to poison grew stronger. He experimented on various products used for anything from flies to aphids. He felt if anything these may make him sick, but nothing worse. He was wrong. He got hold of some highly toxic rat poison.

By this time Robert was not washing his tongue when he put stuff on it. In some cases he would drink a small amount for the effect. He woke up afterwards in and out of consciousness and hooked up to life-support systems in the local hospital. He died two weeks later.

A compulsion of this type is hard to understand, however it does exist. Like other forms of this behavior, it can be cured by professional help. The first step, of course, is for one to admit to having a problem.

*****

Fear and fascination for fire

Pyromania is a fascination for fire. It often starts in early childhood and grows as time goes on. Any number of reasons can cause this. Something as simple as fascination watching a wood-burning fireplace, to being caught in a home fire, can start the problem.

Leslie Adams was five years old when his father stopped to help somebody whose car was on fire. A motorist watching the fire from the highway ran into the back of the car he was in. It burst into flames and almost cost him and his mother their lives. From that time on he had an obsession for fire. He could often be seen walking across the parking lot striking matches and dropping them.

As he grew older the obsession became stronger. He studied fire science in school and got a job with the fire department when he graduated. He could often be seen by his fellow firefighters, staring at the fires as they burned. When needing someone to run in and rescue somebody, Leslie was always the first to volunteer. He had several commendations for this. In truth, the closer he could get to the fire, the better he felt. Although afraid of them, he reasoned that being near them was the only way to overcome that fear.

This obsession almost cost him his life on more than one occasion. When psychiatric trials for various departments were started, this compulsion raised its ugly head. Leslie was ordered to report to the department psychiatrist for a full evaluation. His compulsion slowly receded within the two months he was seeing the doctor. He has now returned to fighting fires, but with an entirely different perspective on them.

*****

Pamela Watson had an aversion to fires and was scared to death of them as a child. This turned to fascination as she grew older. It was not unusual for her to sit on a sofa, eyes glued to a fire burning in the fireplace. She made a game out of seeing how close she could get her hand to the flame without burning it. This caused her many painful mishaps.

Unfortunately this obsession turned cruel. When her parents were away, and nobody was around, she would bring a captured animal, usually a cat or bird to the backyard. There she would douse them with gasoline and set them on fire. No bird could make it over a foot off the ground before succumbing. Cats would often scurry away, starting fires as they would run through a field of brush. The fire department was frequently called to put out these brushfires.

Pamela was finally caught by a hiker on the path behind her home. She was sixteen years old at the time. She was chastised by the judge as well as her parents and ordered to have psychiatric evaluations and treatments. She was also required to do a hundred hours of community service, which she would complete after sessions with the psychiatrist.

Pyromania is a phobia suffered by many of our firefighters. It is an obsession which can be caused by almost anything dealing with fire. When, as a child, one sees devastation it can easily scar them for life. This is especially true if a child is in a burning building or automobile. Some of these people spend time in the hospital from their injuries. Like most compulsions it can be controlled through medicine as well as psychiatric care.

*****

Whipping

Flagellomania is the desire to be whipped, or to whip somebody. These people are referred to as flagellants. This was a religious ritual of the Catholic Church during the thirteenth and into the fourteenth centuries. The church later condemned the practice.

Self-whippings were, and still are penance performed on oneself for perceived sins. They are still commonplace in the Philippines, Mexico, and the Mideast (the practice is illegal in Saudi Arabia.) And in parts the United States.

The flogging of women is legal and commonplace in Middle Eastern countries. Women are given up to thirty lashes, depending on their crime and their ability to withstand such punishment. Any more than that will probably kill the victim. In men the number is higher.

Spankings, and sometimes whippings are common methods of foreplay in some couples. Sadists, usually men, get sexual pleasure from committing this. Masochists, usually women, don't always get perverse pleasure from receiving pain of this nature.

Pietro and Sadie live in the Midwestern town of Lawrenceville. They were attracted to each other through a wife swapping club that specialized in Sadomasochistic practices. Sadie left her husband for

Pietro because of his desires. Unfortunately, because of his habits, he cannot perform his husbandly duties unless inflicting pain on his partner.

She on the other hand cannot get off without this sort of discipline. Handcuffs and masks do not give them added pleasure as in many other couples.

Larry and Betty have a much more involved relationship. Her pleasure comes from being helpless. Larry will often handcuff her to the bed and proceeded to spank her bare bottom. Once it becomes a bright shade of red, and her tears become real, he stops and releases her bonds. At that point they proceed to have sex with each other.

One of the worst examples is with an unwilling partner. Nadine was on her way home from work one night when she was viciously attacked near her home. Leslie was a tattooed monster. His joy came from seeing suffering and horror on the part of his victims. Nadine was dragged to a cellar where she was savagely beaten with a whip and then raped. She died from her wounds. Leslie put her in the trunk of his car and drove into a wooded area where he proceeded to bury her body.

She was his tenth victim. Police were out in force looking for him; however had nothing to go on. His burial sites were all over. Dog handlers with the police department were out daily looking for his victims. His attack on Umami was his last. Unfortunately Leslie was caught in the act of procuring her by James, her husband. He grabbed the whip beating Leslie to death with it. His cries and streams of tears did nothing to stop his torture.

James case was ruled justifiable and he was released without incident. Any other verdict in his case probably would've caused riots. A jury of his peers found him not guilty, unanimously.

*****

Karina and her husband Damien had a good marriage. They both enjoyed their playful past times. Karina was the sadist and Damien the masochist. He got a kick out of being stripped naked and bound with rope on the bed frame with his legs spread apart and bound as well. She would then proceed to lightly whip his scrotum and penis and then bring welts to his back and buttocks. This type of behavior seems odd to most, except those with the same fetishes. Neither ever felt the desire to do this to anybody else.

Flagellation has been going on for centuries. It was used mostly for punishment and, or to get information out of a victim by their captor. Men or women would be taken into a room, stripped and flogged. The most notorious of these rooms was the Tower of London, which also included the rack, where men were stretched and in some cases pulled apart by horses In the courtyard. The Iron Maiden, which tortured and killed many of its victims by spears when its door was closed, was also popular. This form of torture has been used worldwide.

Many people living in England during the eighteenth and nineteenth centuries got a thrill out of watching prisoners be flogged. Many of these people also enjoyed watching victims being drawn and quartered, disemboweling the victim. This was probably the worst form of torture ever conceived by man.

When criminal punishment involved flogging, the man, or woman, would be taken out to the public square. Here they would be stripped to the waist and whipped a given number of lashes, depending on the crime they had committed. This was a common form of punishment.

*****

Fascination with religion

A Theomaniac is a person going beyond religious beliefs. In this condition the man, or woman, believes they are God, or sometimes messengers of God. This is seen all too often in religious cults. Their followers are the type of people who can be easily swayed. Some of these cults number in the hundreds of members and more.

Probably the most notorious of these was "The Reverend James Jones". His congregation originated in Indiana. In the late 50s he attended a University in Indiana. There he grew a fascination for Mahatma Gandhi, Karl Marx, Joseph Stalin and Adolf Hitler. He began an underground movement towards Marxism in the United States. At that point he became an avowed communist.

He was put under tighter scrutiny, when government officials started looking into his business dealings, after moving his cult to San Francisco in the early 70s. He had the full support of city government. George Moscone, then Mayor, elected him as head of the housing projects. He had the full support of then-President Jimmy Carter. Jones organization came to be called the People's Temple.

When news stories came out about physical, mental and sexual abuse taking place, Jones pulled up stakes and moved to Jonestown

Guyana, a compound they had started building in the early 70s. Over nine hundred of his followers moved there. He looked at this as a communist haven and like too many dictators in history, would not allow anybody to leave the compound.

In 1978 the United States government sent five emissaries including Congressman Leo Ryan, to make a report on their activities. He was attacked with a knife by one of Jones rookies. After their visit they, along with fifteen people wishing to defect, were taken to nearby Port Kaituma airstrip. Before boarding the plane they were all killed by the drivers of pickup trucks that came into the airport at Jones orders.

Jim Jones' drug addiction convinced him he was God. In 1978 all the men women and children were poisoned as well as Jones himself. He had his followers convinced that upon their death there would be a "translation" to another planet. Jones had shot himself in the head as well.

A religious sect of the Seventh-day Adventist church, calling themselves the Branch Dravidians, predicted the end of the world in 1969. They based this apocalypse on a prophecy of the second coming of Christ. When that Armageddon failed to materialize, they moved to

Elk County, Texas. Vernon Howell became the leader after the death of its founder, Victor Houteff. The group moved its headquarters to mount caramel, east of Waco. As the group began to grow, they moved to a larger piece of land nearby.

Vernon Howell took the name, David Koresh. He felt he was the Messiah as he had been groomed for that position by Lois Rodin, whose husband had originally started the sect. The Department of Alcohol, Tobacco and Firearms got wind of weapons being stored at the compound. They didn't feel the firearms were illegal, but they heard that the guns were being transformed into illegal weapons. The ATF (Bureau of Alcohol Tobacco and Firearms) tried for two days to gain entrance. When that failed the FBI was called in.

Stories very as to whether the FBI or the Dravidians' themselves were responsible for a fire that ensued when the authorities tried to gain entrance to the compound. There had been several accusations of sexual abuse and child endangerment. When all was said and done, seventy-six people, including women and children, died. David Koresh was also one of the victims.

*****

Jeremiah Smith had a cult of supporters in the middle of the Arizona desert, near Mesa. Members numbered in the hundreds. He had set up a regular city, which he named Smithville. The cult was totally self-sufficient. Being an astute speaker, he was able to convince his followers that he was a messenger from God. At a later date he would become God. Religious services were held every night and everyone was ordered to attend. In order to become a member of this group, one had to sign over all their belongings.

This sect was not an off-shoot of any other religion, but rather one of their own. The Bible was considered heresy, and the world's religions were shunned. All was well until Jeremiah started to go against his own preaching's. He'd taken several wives and now felt it his responsibility to deflower the young girls being raised there, as well as having them bear his children.

Although the parents of these children have been brainwashed, parental instinct came into play. The father of one of the girls was able to make his way to a convenience store several miles away, where he called police and told them what was going on.

The next morning agents from social services and police officers came into the compound and arrested Smith without incident.

Affidavits from the girl's parents, as well as on the spot medical examinations, proved the allegations to be correct. Smith was tried and convicted on fifteen counts of first-degree rape. The property, in which the compound sat, was sold and the money returned to the people. Smith was given twenty years in Arizona State prison.

From back as far as recorded history, men have tried to set themselves up as God's. The pharaohs in ancient Egypt were a prime example. As the king would, upon his death, be replaced by a successor, usually a son, that successor was considered a deity. The people worshiped God's of the sun, moon, and stars. In ancient culture was the belief, chariots of these gods would appear.

Throughout history, many rulers of countries would set themselves up as God, and be worshiped by the people. They were taught to believe and obey the wishes of these puppet dictators.

Many religions of today teach their followers to pay for their way to heaven. This is done through tithes to the church and the corporations that run them. Since the beginning of time death has always been big business and will continue to be in the future.

The End.

Reg. U.S copyright office.

Copyright #1-1943052741

Look for other titles by Daniel Henderson through Amazon.com.

www.ingramcontent.com/pod-product-compliance
Lightning Source LLC
Chambersburg PA
CBHW080243290526
45790CB00005B/1683